Praying the
Jesus Prayer Together

Praying the
Jesus Prayer Together

Lord Jesus Christ,
Son of God,
have mercy on me,
a sinner.

BROTHER RAMON
&
SIMON BARRINGTON-WARD

Published by
The Bible Reading Fellowship
First Floor, Elsfield Hall
15–17 Elsfield Way, Oxford OX2 8FG
ISBN 1 84101 147 9

First published 2001
1 3 5 7 9 10 8 6 4 2 0
All rights reserved

Acknowledgments
Unless otherwise stated, scripture quotations are taken from The New
Revised Standard Version of the Bible, Anglicized Edition, copyright ©
1989, 1995 by the Division of Christian Education of the National
Council of the Churches of Christ in the USA, and are used by
permission. All rights reserved.

Scripture quotations taken from the Holy Bible, New International
Version, copyright © 1973, 1978, 1984 by International Bible Society,
are used by permission of Hodder & Stoughton Limited. All rights
reserved. 'NIV' is a registered trademark of International Bible Society.
UK trademark number 1448790.

Extracts from the Authorized Version of the Bible (The King James Bible),
the rights in which are vested in the Crown, are reproduced by
permission of the Crown's patentee, Cambridge University Press.

p. 114 Extract from 'The Lord's Prayer' ('The Millennium Prayer') by
Paul Field and Stephen Deal, copyright © 1998 Meadowgreen Music/
EMI Christian Music Publishing/Stephen Deal Music. Administered by
CopyCare, PO Box 77, BN27 3EF. Used by permission.
music@copycare.com

A catalogue record for this book is available from the British Library

Printed and bound in Great Britain by
Omnia Books Limited, Glasgow

Contents

THE DYNAMIC OF THE JESUS PRAYER

Can you imagine two groups of people in whom something gentle, interior and yet very powerful is taking place? Something dynamic. *Dynamis* (the New Testament word from which our 'dynamite' comes) indicates the dynamic healing and life-giving power that flowed from Jesus in his ministry, revitalizing the spiritual and physical life of those who looked to him in faith and touched him in yearning. It is the opposite of a static and cerebral religion that has no power to move, bless or give life.

What I am talking about is two groups of people who have recently been introduced to the Jesus Prayer, which is an ancient yet simple form of contemplative prayer, rooted in scripture. Over the last few decades it has spread out of the Eastern Orthodox tradition and into the lives and spirituality of Western Christians, causing a quiet revolution.

The first group of people consists of about twenty ordinary men and women, young and old, who have recently completed an experimental retreat on the Jesus Prayer conducted by Bishop Simon Barrington-Ward (hereafter Bishop Simon). They are from the mainline denominations, with a sprinkling of those disappointed or disillusioned with what they have previously found, and looking for a spirituality which is both objectively based and which will meet their spiritual needs.

During the weekend they learned *how* to pray in a new, simple and dynamic way, involving mind, heart and body in a holistic and joyful teaching. They had previously been told, over many years, about the definitions of prayer, the importance of prayer, the value of prayer and the necessity of prayer for a healthy, spiritual life, but no one had told them or shown them just how to do it. The whole dimension of the body – the physical, the sensory – was omitted, and this left them wondering what it was really about, and if it was actually possible. So they left it to the monks, nuns and other 'prayer professionals'.

Then, during that weekend, the majority of these ordinary people were actually learning it, doing it, feeling it. Something was actually going on within their own being and in their daily lives. And they suspected that if they continued this newly learned practice, not depending on feelings but on solid faith, they would break through into a new way not only of praying, but of being – alone and together.

The second group consists of a company of novices, with a sprinkling of university students who had participated in a teaching week on the Jesus Prayer led by Brother Ramon SSF. After the week, they found themselves plunged back into university and secular life or, in the case of the novices, doing prison, chaplain, hospital or parish work, or simply caught up in their ongoing life-commitment in their various religious houses or monasteries. But the Jesus Prayer was still doing its work under God – buzzing, moving, stirring, affecting all those who entered wholeheartedly into the retreats. And that is what this book is all about – inviting individuals and groups to come into a new experience of prayer through using the Jesus Prayer.

Both of us, Brother Ramon and Bishop Simon, are indebted to the Eastern Orthodox Monastery at Tolleshunt Knights, Essex, for our warm reception and fellowship with the community there. They are not responsible for any misunderstanding (or heresy!) of ours that may have crept into this book, but we do acknowledge our debt of teaching and joy.

We have both been practising and teaching the Jesus Prayer for well over twenty years, and it has become the mainstay of our private and teaching prayer. At the same time we acknowledge the necessity for a full sacramental and Bible-rooted life of liturgy and affirmation within the Church of God as the context in which it needs to take place.

We invite you into the pages of this book, into the joy of the Jesus Prayer, and into a fuller, deeper life in Christ – for the world, for the Church and to the praise and glory of God, Father, Son and Holy Spirit.

Brother Ramon SSF
Bishop Simon Barrington-Ward

CHAPTER 1

WEEK OF GLORY

Brother Ramon writes:

I had known of Bishop Simon for many years, mainly as General Secretary of the Church Mission Society and as Bishop of Coventry, and was always stirred by his pilgrimage in which he was at home in the evangelical and catholic traditions of the Church of God, with a human openness and lack of exclusivity that reflected Jesus his Lord and Saviour.

When I recognized his increasing appreciation of the Eastern Orthodox tradition, and especially his teaching on the Jesus Prayer (we had both written books on the subject) I was stirred by what I understood to be the Holy Spirit causing me to invite him to Glasshampton Monastery, where I was testing my deeper vocation to the hermit life during the early 1990s.

Our meeting confirmed in us both that it was surely of the Holy Spirit, and this led us to set up a meeting of the inside of a week, the mornings of which would be devoted to the practice, teaching and sharing of the Jesus Prayer—how we could deepen its influence and work in our own lives, and whether or not we might be called upon to share our findings under the guidance of the Spirit who was so moving us.

I've called this a 'week of glory' and so it was. But it was also a time during which I experienced a participation in physical pain and darkness. I shall deal with that in a later chapter, but here I want to talk about the glory and wonder of what we experienced and learned together. The Lord graciously gave me relative freedom from such pain and darkness during the necessary mornings, though our afternoons worked out differently—and that was part of the pattern too.

The morning mechanics worked out like this: Bishop Simon came down to my hermitage enclosure and we prayed the Jesus Prayer in my Prayer Hut, verbally, rhythmically, for the 100 knots of the prayer rope (some mornings in English and some in Greek). And then we entered into silence, completing the hour.

Then we retired to my Living Hut for coffee, and during the next hour shared in conversation, reflection and wonder over the theological and spiritual implications of the prayer in our lives and teaching. This was not a psychological exercise but a seeking after God in response to the Spirit's invitation.

Some mornings it resulted in quiet reflection, but this was mingled with sheer joy in the quality and power of the reverberations struck within our souls. And there was also that sane, simple gentleness which 'expected nothing' and was content with what was given.

Then we separated until the next morning, allowing the Lord to work within us the power of it all. For Bishop Simon, he will indicate how the time was for him, but for me the afternoons especially were a mingling of joy and physical pain, for I was in the middle of coming to terms with the onset of pelvic pain, albeit relieved and controlled somewhat by the sterling work of the Macmillan nurse. And I can rejoice for the respite of my present vantage point, as I write. Yet that also is directly relevant to my continued practice of the Jesus Prayer, and carries me still deeper into the mystical love and healing power of God.

There is much to say about the healing power mediated through this kind of praying, but it certainly does not lend itself to some slick or quick solution. It is, rather, about living at the basic depth of your humanity, entering into the ecstatic and despairing places of the human person and remaining there for oneself, for others, for the world and for the glory and wonder of God. I constantly ponder on the words of St Silouan the Athonite when he wrote about descending into hell, remaining there and despairing not.

Hermit and bishop together

When choosing a title for this book, it seemed that the 'together' word was important, not just because it is significant that a bishop and hermit from the Anglican tradition could be and pray together with great joy and dynamic, and represent both the evangelical and catholic dimensions of the faith and love of Christ, but because God had moved us together. He had given us great joy in one another and was taking us deeper through the Jesus Prayer—and now stirring us up to share further what he was showing us

We are both very bold, therefore (though the Lord humbles us along the way), to say: 'Come on in—dig for the treasure, seek for the pearl, look for the lost coin.'

Our boldness is not an exclusive claim, for we are only servants of our Lord, and we belong to a struggling, failing and poor part of the Church, yet one in which the fullness of the gospel may be found. We also acknowledge duly, gladly and gratefully the dynamic tradition of the Eastern Orthodox Church, with its ancient roots and contemporary renewed spirituality. And on the way we share with the great Roman Church of the West and with our fellow Christians within the Reformed traditions.

It is not our task to persuade you to take all this on board, but we believe it is part of our joyful mission to share what has been shared with us—and that includes the life-giving practice of the Jesus Prayer—for our own fellowship continues and deepens.

Bishop Simon writes:

Homecoming to Brother Ramon's hermitage

Sometimes you step across a particular threshold, you meet with a particular person in a particular place, and you know that this encounter has some kind of special and lasting meaning. Something is happening that you will always remember. You are sensing the reality, the goal towards which all life is moving. In this happening, at this particular moment, you find yourself in a setting that is suddenly as vivid and radiant and clear as an illumination in a Book of Hours. You are glimpsing something of that wholeness which is our true destiny, our own ultimate homecoming and that of the whole creation.

I remember realizing that this was what had happened on visits to Brother Ramon, a remarkable Anglican Franciscan, who was living out his vocation to the solitary life. I was thinking about this as I drove along on my way to a further visit. Now he had asked me to come with him into a special exploration of a way of prayer that had been given to us both, out of the very heart of the earliest Christian communities. It was the so-called 'Jesus Prayer'.

This way of praying had come to us as a persistent stream of the Spirit, making its first known appearance in the Egyptian or Syrian deserts at the time of Constantine, and then flowing on underground, sometimes hidden, sometimes emerging, through centuries of Eastern and Russian Christendom. It flowed through the lives and writings of often obscure people, in a desert or in a remote wilderness or mountain, including eventually the 'holy mountain', Mount Athos; or in the depths of the great forests, in hermitages, in little hut settlements, in monastic communities and latterly in concentration camps and gulags.

When the stream finally touched people in the West in the 1920s, they recognized that parallel tributaries from the same source had nourished the witness of our own teachers of prayer. I had dared to put something about this Eastern tradition on paper in a little book, one of many on this subject, called *The Jesus Prayer* (BRF, 1996). Brother Ramon, in his own pilgrimage, had drawn more deeply than I upon this stream already, and now, after I had made three visits to his hermitage, he had invited me to come and attempt to merge my quest with his. We were to pray the Prayer together over a week.

I knew as I drew closer to his hermitage (at Glasshampton in Worcestershire) that this stage of the journey had now become, for me as for many, a very special sequence. I had made it in autumn and in summer, on my own and then with my wife and with our dog, Holly, whom Ramon had spotted in the back of the car and invited us to bring in with us! We were just two (or three) out of a range of other seekers who had arrived in the same way, young hippies or 'New Agers', older agnostic inquirers, or just ordinary church members in search of something more.

There was always that moment when you reached the hill country and then, having gone steeply down, just beyond a bridge, you would come upon that turning, unexpected and obscure, a rough track, not apparently going anywhere. After you had made your bumpy way along it, slowly, upwards through trees and past a wood, you went on climbing. Then, nearer the top, there would suddenly come into view the surprising front of a great, handsome, stable-block, completely on its own, high over the countryside, looking as if it had come to rest on its hilltop like Noah's ark after the flood. Below the clock tower, startlingly, are inscribed the unexpected words, 'There stood at the Cross of Jesus, Mary his Mother.'

This stable-block in fact was left here after a fire had destroyed the great house it was built to serve. After a century and a half, an Anglican priest had arrived, striving to start a community here that would pray in 'quietness, hiddenness and simplicity'. And when no one would stay with him he eventually died in 1937, feeling he had failed. He never knew that the Franciscans would fulfil something of his isolated vision, by using the place to train their own brothers to pray and by receiving others there who came in need of silent retreat and contemplation.

After worship with the brothers in the main house, and sometimes after a meal, I would be led through a long passage and out by way of a pantry that opened on to a well-kept vegetable garden tended by Brother Ramon.

Raymond (Ramon's baptismal name) had grown up as a Baptist, become a Baptist minister, then an Anglican and, after a time of study, first a curate and then a parish priest and after that a university chaplain. He spent a year with a little monastic community in Scotland at Roslin. After this he became an Anglican Franciscan, Brother 'Ramon', (the name of a great Franciscan mystic and missionary of the Middle Ages), joining in this Order's ministry of evangelism and mission. But then he felt the calling to withdraw to pray in solitude for six months at a time, first in Dorset and next on the edge of the Lleyn peninsula in his native Wales.

From there he was to come to this very place, the stable-block on the hill, to be 'Guardian' as the Franciscans call the presiding brother, teaching novices and helping brothers and visitors to pray. But the deep urge to return to the solitary life welled up in him. After six years he withdrew to the grounds of Ty Mawr, a convent in Wales, where he spent two more years in a small caravan, freezing in winter, until he was compelled to give up under doctor's orders. Then he felt the Spirit summoning him back to this hill, to three huts beyond the garden, there to pray, later to write, and to receive a few visitors at times, and thus to be a kind of flying buttress to his old community, working out a new relationship with them.

Once you passed through a door set within the thick hedge that surrounded his enclosure, you struck a large bell that hung beside you. Then, in a moment, from out behind the huts to the side of you, Brother Ramon appeared as if by magic. His letters had been vivid and enthusiastic and welcoming. But it was still with a shock of surprise that I had first met this immediately warm and genial figure, in his brown habit with its white knotted cord, a figure so solidly planted on this earth, so jovial, rubicund, and full of life and laughter as though already we were in the middle of a party! Somehow he seemed essentially gregarious and convivial. How did this go with the lonely discipline of a hermit, the deep-laid, hidden search for God?

There was no seeming reserve about him. His talk, like his writing, bubbled up, the Welsh tones adding a rush and sparkle. He immediately shared his story and evoked from you your own. He gave you all that had just been happening in his heart and mind and encouraged you to respond with the same freedom.

The first time I met him, as he welcomed me joyfully, laying his hands on my shoulders, I was reminded of a small plaque of St Francis joyfully greeting St Dominic at their legendary meeting which stands in its alcove in my little study/chapel at home. There was something very definitely of a Welsh St Francis about Ramon. The person he was embracing on this occasion with such character-istic affection was, alas, no Dominic. But his delighted welcome lifted me out of my own sense of inadequacy, as one embodying (as I knew I did, as a bishop), the contradictions and the longings and frustrations of the Church, of so many religious and secular institutions, of the world and also of the all-too-human heart. He seemed to be both accepting of our incongruities and laughing at them, his own as well as mine, in the light of a mercy that both showed them up and healed them.

As with St Francis, Ramon's unfeigned pleasure that I had come led us into the sheer ease of talking freely with each other about what mattered most to both of us, exchanging our concerns and our discoveries, and entering into the sheer excitement and joy that seemed to irradiate the exchange. Through a gap in the hedge, I could look out over fields, freshly ploughed on my first visit, thick with corn on the next—fields that ran down into a valley and up on the other side to where the distant red tower of a church crowned the far hill.

On the last visit I had made, with my wife, we had laughed and talked together as we sat in Ramon's Living Hut. He fetched an icon to give us that he had made next door in his Workshop Hut and pulled out one of the many books he had written to inscribe it and hand it to us. He did this on my every visit! Then we went into his third hut, which was his chapel, and there we prayed together in silence on stools in front of the small altar and the St Francis' crucifix, a replica of the one that had hung in the little church of San Damiano in Assisi for centuries before Christ spoke from it to Francis as he knelt there.

On these occasions I cannot remember much of what happened in the praying in Ramon's Prayer Hut. I am sure that there and then we were seeking to use the Jesus Prayer 'with the mind in the heart', as, in Eastern tradition, those who used and wrote about this way of praying had put it. This meant saying the actual words of the Prayer, 'Lord Jesus Christ Son of God have mercy upon me, a sinner', in such a way that you *feel* it as well as thinking it—what T.S. Eliot called 'thinking your feelings and feeling your thoughts'. This always, for me, had come more easily than usual when I was with Ramon, because alongside him I always found such a strong awareness of the reality of the living God. To kneel before his wonderful icon cross was to be brought nearer to St Francis in San Damiano, and thus to be given a strong awareness that you were kneeling before the living Christ, crucified and risen. The voice that spoke to Francis then might even speak to our hearts now. The Jesus Prayer itself is essentially, as Ramon and I agreed, simply the 'practice of the presence of Christ'. And there are few places where I have felt that presence more strongly than in Ramon's Prayer Hut.

That sense of presence is in itself a homecoming of a kind that gives you a hint of things to come, 'a breath from a far country' (C.S. Lewis). All the things around you, the hedges, the fields, the distant tower, become intensely alive and distinct and yet all held in one. You seem almost to have arrived closer to the fulfilment of all life. But then, as always in this time of waiting, the eternal moment ends. The sadness of saying goodbye is intensified by a definite sense of loss and of being woken into that strange dream which we call 'reality'.

Even Holly, our dog, while we went into the Prayer Hut, had gone *underneath* it. (The hut was raised on stilts from the ground to protect its floor.) Holly lay there so still that it took a while to find her. Ramon was amused by my efforts to extract her! He urged me to let her be. It didn't even seem to be special smells that were keeping her, but just a kind of contentment. She was obviously as happy to be there with him as we were, and she didn't want to leave. But the time had to come. As we drove away, we knew that we were still elated and borne along on some kind of current of the Spirit that would continue to carry us for some time to come. The two abiding memories of any visit to Ramon were the stillness and the laughter.

Journeying with Brother Ramon

So you can imagine how excited I was at the thought of being about to spend the inside of a week in that Franciscan monastery. I would be joining in the community prayers in the main chapel in the early morning. This was a lovely cavern of a place in the heart of the old stables. From the far wall, a sculpted Christ leans out from his cross as if to draw your faint worship and your small intercessions up into his unfathomable self-offering.

Then I would go down each day to spend time praying the Jesus Prayer with Ramon in his Prayer Hut. Afterwards we would repair to his Living Hut to reflect on what we had received, and to drink a cup of coffee together. I felt sure that the Spirit was going to give us some new insight into the meaning of God in Christ for us.

The first hint I had that all might not be quite the same as in the past had come some months earlier, when Ramon had written to say that he had been discovered to have prostate cancer and was receiving an excellent new hormone treatment. He had received special prayer and anointing from a good friend, surrounded by the community of his brothers. He was looking for and trusting in the possibility of complete healing. But when I later rang to confirm the date of my coming, Brother Raymond Christian, the member of the community responsible for guests, told me that I would find Ramon quite a bit changed and revealed that he was suffering from a good deal of pain after recently needing further treatment. Ramon had written little about this and had done nothing to cancel my coming. He was so eager that we should share this experience of the Prayer and perhaps write about it—the hermit and the bishop together, an idea that greatly appealed to him. He kept mentioning it!

So it came about that, after I had received the usual kindly evening welcome into the main house and been able to prepare quietly, I went down to Ramon's enclosure the next morning after worship and breakfast with the community. A little tremulously, I struck the bell inside the gate. He called out that he was just coming and soon appeared. I need not have worried, in one way. He was as joyfully and lovingly welcoming as ever. But his colour had largely gone. He was his old self, but strikingly pale, and now limping noticeably. He made little of this but eagerly led me at once into the Prayer Hut.

We then followed the same pattern each morning for the inside of a week. We would begin by sitting on a low bench and talking together for a while about what we were going to do, in a way that became in itself a kind of shared meditation. Then we would move to two prayer stools in front of the small altar and the crucifix. I could see that Ramon had difficulty in adjusting to this, since he was clearly in pain, but he soon settled into it in his usual way. And we would gather ourselves together in silence, settling into stillness and letting our breathing become slower and deeper.

On the first morning, I spoke the Prayer aloud. The second morning he did. We would always begin the Prayer with an invocation of the Holy Spirit. Ramon mentioned that the tuft of wool on the end of the Orthodox 'prayer rope' could be seen as a symbol of

Pentecost, of the Spirit opened up to us by the cross itself and drawing us through the cross into the life of the Trinity. So we would take our prayer ropes and hold that tuft between thumb and forefinger as we began with an invocation of the Holy Spirit. Then, as the Prayer was spoken, with each saying of it, we took hold of each knot in turn round the rope until we came back to the start. There we would end with 'Lord Jesus Christ, Son of God,' emphasizing that we began and ended with him, the Alpha and the Omega. After a pause and a further prayer and silence, we would go back to Ramon's Living Hut.

On the last two mornings we both said the Prayer together, saying it, at Ramon's suggestion, in Greek. The prayer fell easily into a kind of rhythm of three beats: 'Lord Jesus Christ, or 'Kyrie Jesu Christe; then two: 'Son of God' or 'huie tou Theou'; and then three again: 'Have mercy upon us!' or 'ele-i-son hemas.' (You could, if you found it helpful, breathe in on the first three, hold your breath for the middle two and release it again with the last three, but that's very much an optional extra!)

I found that saying the prayer in Greek greatly reinforced the immediacy and directness that Ramon's own Franciscan style and indeed the San Damiano crucifix itself had already given us. Suddenly, praying in the language used by the writers of the Gospels and by many of those who first used this kind of prayer in their huts in the desert, and also being together in Ramon's little hut, seemed to intensify the strong sense of being brought near to those who in the Gospels cried out in the same kind of words as those of the Jesus Prayer and through them were brought near to Jesus This was the 'practice of the presence' indeed!

But there was a vast difference between this time and any that I had enjoyed with Ramon there before. I could see that Ramon, even though he had taken painkillers, was struggling with the ache in his side. Though he made light of it, he was being weakened by it. A shadow was over us even as we launched out each morning, which increased the feeling that we were venturing into uncharted waters.

Ramon remarked as we sat in his Prayer Hut together on the first morning, our prayer ropes in our hands, that it was as if we were in an absurd little boat about to voyage out into the great deep. I mentioned that when my elder daughter, then not quite five, was about to set off for her school for the first time ever, a friend of ours had given her an inscription to go on the wall above her bed. It was the Breton fisherman's prayer, 'O God be good to me! The sea is so wide and my boat is so small.' And Ramon reminded me of how Stephen, a priest from my own diocese whom we both held dear, had once, before he was ordained, at a time when he was still very much a seeker, come to stay a few nights in this actual hut, to pray on his own. On the first night a storm blew up. Stephen dreamt that he was lost in wild waters until at length a little child came and gently took his hand and drew him back to home and safety. The child in him and in each of us, and the Christ-child perhaps...

Even when Ramon had been well, he had never denied his consciousness of his own weaknesses. We emphasized now to each other that we both knew ourselves to be sinful people constantly in need of help, precarious and vulnerable, wanting just to give ourselves to steadfast ordinary prayer, not expecting anything spectacular or dramatic! Ramon had always been frank both in writing and talk about his consciousness of perhaps being too much 'on an ego trip', as he rather severely put it—almost too fluent in speech and writing, 'flying off in too many directions'. I could identify with that. He knew that his very gifts of relating so instantly and vividly to all kinds of people and bringing alive to them the experiences of the Spirit they already had, his impulsive responsiveness and enthusiasm, had often needed to be offered up to God and submitted to a profound discipline and obedience. This was all part of our journey together now.

On those mornings, as we voyaged further, I began to sense a powerful current, that deep thrust towards silence and solitude that underlay Ramon's marvellous capacity for conviviality and fun. The Jesus Prayer itself is a departure from all words and concepts.

The Prayer enables you to keep moving towards a greater silence. The Orthodox tradition calls it *hesychia*, the stilling of all 'thoughts' (*logismoi*). You have to learn to keep guarding against and excluding these! You have to keep turning away from endless distracting byways; to go on being drawn into the plea 'Lord Jesus Christ, Son of God', to 'let the name of Jesus accompany your every breath', as John Climacus put it. (He was the sixth/seventh-century monk and abbot of the great monastery on the side of Mount Sinai who drew together the traditions of prayer of the first centuries in his famous book *The Ladder*). You have to keep recovering that simple attempt, leaving all else behind you, to turn deeply into the quest for the presence, for that love unknown which is beyond all image or thought. To emphasize this, Ramon and I always ended with a period of silence.

I had already had the feeling when I was praying with him of a further pull, flowing underneath all our talk and laughter, of a profound, far-reaching compassion for all those for whom he would intercede, for the sick, the multitudes of the poor and the oppressed peoples of the 'Two-Thirds' world and here in the West—people so much forgotten by the rest of us. Within that intercession was an immense, almost lonely hunger and thirst, on behalf both of himself and of our world, a longing in the depths of his being for the living God. This was the driving force behind his quest for solitude.

But now this ever-present stream had widened into a flood. His joy and his spontaneous sense of fun were as great as ever, and so was his delight in what we were doing together. But it seemed, as when the lights on a vessel setting out at sunset gleam more sharply over the darkening waters, to shine out within some overall closing in of the dark. I had an inkling that he had now half given up the prospect of a miraculous healing in this life. Somehow he seemed to be seeing himself as already turned towards a greater light on the other side of darkness. The wholeness we had felt so vividly on our visits to him was not gone. But perhaps it was now clearer that it was just a hint of what could be reached only beyond the present horizon, only through a further brokenness. The earlier yearning for solitude was opening out into a wider yearning for a still greater surrender of himself, with a readiness for whatever the divine Love might have in store for him.

Our labouring away together to enter through the Jesus Prayer 'into the presence' was being strangely rewarded beyond any expectation morning by morning. After each hour together, we went back into Ramon's Living Hut to sit and reflect on what was coming to us.

Somehow, even when I was praying, and for long afterwards, the San Damiano crucifix glowed on in my memory as a bright light can do after you have closed your eyes. Indeed, in praying the Jesus Prayer you do close your eyes and seek to be conscious of nothing but God with us—Immanuel, that unseen presence impossible to picture. Yet, for all that, in some subtle way, the crucifix seemed still to inform our praying, as the icons do in an Orthodox church, even when you have closed your eyes.

The One who came to us in the stillness, was the One who had prayed in the hour before his Passion, in the equivalent to Gethsemane in John's story of the Passion: 'What shall I say, "Father save me from this hour?" No, for this purpose I have come to this hour. Father, glorify your name.' His 'hour' in which he was to be glorified was the hour in which he was 'lifted up' on to the cross. In John's account of the Passion, which shaped this crucifix as it shaped so much of the Orthodox tradition from the beginning, the victory begins here. Resurrection, ascension and even Pentecost are already implicit in Christ crucified.

This icon cross was very much an Eastern Orthodox crucifix, as Ramon stressed to me, though how it came as far west as San Damiano in Assisi is a mystery. But this was the form through which Christ spoke to Francis. Here, West and East met. And for the East, the influence of John's Gospel is specially strong. For John, glory and pain are strangely fused, and so in Eastern writings and icons. In the Christ who disclosed himself here to Francis, the crown of glory replaces the crown of thorns. The wound in his side is here as in John's Gospel, releasing forgiveness and healing. All the figures painted on this cross, whom Ramon loved to point out, are figures from John's version of the Passion story.

Here the Christ who gazes from the cross towards you is a youthful warrior, leaping up on to the tree to do battle with the powers of evil. It reminds me of the imagery in the earliest poem in the English language, a Saxon poem carved, Celtic-style, on a *beacn*, a solitary stone pillar, found up on the edge of the then-known world. Its light streams out into the dark ages in Northumbria. The poem thus discovered was called 'A Riddle of a Rood' (a Saxon word used to describe the cross of Christ or a crucifix). In the poem (written among a people who loved riddles), the cross speaks as a tree that asks us to guess what it truly is. Then it gives the answer. It tells how it has become 'the wondrous cross' (as Isaac Watts put it centuries later in his first version of 'When I survey') 'where that *young* Prince of Glory died'. Those were Watts' original words, echoing ancient tradition. I wish we still sang that line like that![1]

The ancient cross both in *A Riddle of a Rood* and in the icon from St Damian's church at Assisi is a glorious cross, like the crucifix a Russian archbishop gave me when I was at Coventry, which is topped by a crown. On that Russian crucifix, as on the St Damian cross in Ramon's Prayer Hut, Christ is shown as both suffering and reigning, dying and triumphing simultaneously. Within the crown of glory on Christ's head in Ramon's cross, there is the outline of a little cross suffused with light. The seashells round the border of this whole crucifix were seen at the time of its painting as a symbol of the beauty and eternity of heaven opened up to us through Christ's Passion.

The gold background and the bright red (symbolizing love) and the other colours of the clothes of the figures of Mary, John and the Roman centurion are bathed in light, as they all stand under Christ's outstretched arms. Underneath his pierced hands, angels gaze at his wounds. Even the two smaller figures, there at each end of the cross-bar—seemingly standing for those who killed Jesus, the Jew and the Gentile—are already 'looking on him whom they pierced'. At the very base of the cross, the upper part of the figures of seekers, drawn to Christ, seems to have been worn away, perhaps by worshippers who, in Orthodox fashion, had kissed the icon reverently through the centuries.

The Christ figure himself gazes with large eyes ('Love with its eyes open') upon us and upon the Father whom he would have us see, and the angels on either side of him gaze steadily at his wounds, by which we are healed. The dove faintly discerned on his forehead shows him as the one in whom the Spirit dwells and through whom that Spirit becomes accessible to all who will be united with him as a living temple. The faintest outline of a person's head on his body suggests the Father seen through him and dwelling in him, and, just below, a circle with a figure within symbolizes the eternal Word, the *logos* made flesh in him. The hint of a veil that covers his crown and his face and neck is like the cloud that veiled the glory of the Lord in Exodus, a veil that will be lifted to those who believe in him— even in this life.

In praying the Jesus Prayer, Ramon, in pain or fatigue, and I through being with him, experienced Christ disclosing himself to us, in glory through woundedness, life through death, power in weakness, more vividly, closely and clearly than we had ever known before. Those who have prayed this prayer through the centuries have claimed again and again that the power of the name of Jesus is restored to them, the sense that in uttering that name in the strength of the Holy Spirit they are brought not only into the presence but into a living communion with God in Christ. And quite gently and strongly, without any great exaltation or drama, we both seemed to recognize the infinite tenderness and severity of such an encounter. Then I realized that the sense of 'homecoming in the Spirit' that I and others had felt on our visits to Ramon in his hermitage, and yet also the awareness of an infinite distance from our true home, were both encountered here in the person of Jesus Christ as nowhere else in heaven or earth.

When Jesus starts his ministry in the Gospel stories (especially in his sudden emergence at the beginning of Mark), he comes proclaiming the nearness of the final 'kingdom' or rule of God. He discloses himself to be the centre of a new Israel, a new kingdom community in which God's love will hold sway, and invites into it all people, especially those apparently shut out from God and his rule. In the first phase of his ministry, in what has been called the 'Galilean spring', he sets up what looks like the preliminary framework for a new society, a new humanity, a new creation even, close at hand and open to everyone, even the most distant and excluded. At special moments such as, for some of us, visits to Ramon in his hermitage, such a possibility seems to be laying hold of us.

But then for Jesus' followers that was all smashed down, dismantled and taken away. Surely no such movement of faith anywhere in any religion has been offered out of such a wholeness followed by such utter brokenness. Yet Jesus then opens up a way through that terrible darkness which seems to close in upon us, disintegrating all our hopes, all our intuitions of a coming fulfilment. Jesus crucified and risen, that suffering yet joyful figure depicted on the cross of St Francis, is the one place anywhere where the final healing and bringing into harmony of all things is held together completely with the present frustration and confusion. In him, the 'then' and the 'now' or the 'not yet' are kept in one.

The Prayer that Ramon and I had been praying, invoking the name of Jesus, brings us into that same integration. Here is a fusion of homecoming and journeying; ultimate just peace (shalom) and present frustration; transcendent love, goodness, holiness and our present mutual oppression and sinfulness; a delicate harmony of all things and at the same time a failing of love, and a loss of order or meaning.

'Lord Jesus Christ...': with every entry into his presence and joy, made at his invitation, bringing us into his welcome and forgiveness and renewing power, we break through again. 'Son of God...': the One who leads us home to the Father brings us back into the all-embracing love of the Trinity. 'Have mercy upon us' becomes 'draw us into oneness with you, cleanse and renew us, that in prayer and action we may be brought into God's continuing healing purpose, more and more'. We find our part in God's redemptive process opened up to us in Christ as we invoke his presence and his name.

Ramon and I were conscious of having been led more deeply into this process by the end of that week together, in a way that neither of us could have arrived at in the same way separately. We saw suddenly the strength of a united movement of prayer, rooted in Christ and in the Holy Spirit, gathered up into one rhythm and theme. Here is given to each one of us a God for the Godless, a prayer for the prayerless, an entry point into the very heart of history for those who may feel themselves far outside any hope of homecoming, a door like the 'little, stiff, darkened door' through which Columba hoped somehow to enter heaven! Here was an unexpected entry point set right alongside the furthest and most distant of us, even at our darkest moments, an entry into a way leading through and beyond our tragedy into an infinite, shared joy.

CHAPTER 2

THE JESUS PRAYER AS LIFE THROUGH DEATH: A LAST VISIT TO RAMON

Bishop Simon writes:

After that amazing week, life was not the same. For me in my attic study chapel in Cambridge, the prayer deepened and quickened. I had in front of me on my 'altar' (a simple, carved wooden chest from Nigeria), on a plain wooden stand made originally by a dear friend for Ramon, the text of the Jesus Prayer that Ramon had inscribed for me in Greek. Not surprisingly, as I knelt on a prayer stool there saying the Prayer in front of the icons, I prayed often with and for Ramon. But I also often had an uncanny sense that we were still together in his Prayer Hut and that he was beside me as I prayed. After 'Lord Jesus Christ, Son of God' (*Kyrie Jesu Christe huie tou Theou*) I usually use the words 'have mercy on me, a sinner' in the second part of the Prayer (*eleison me ton hamartohlon*—literally 'the sinner'). But when I felt we were there together in Christ's presence, I found myself saying '*eleison hemas*' (have mercy upon us). We were still saying the Prayer together, as indeed, in a true sense, those who pray this Prayer always are.

During this time, Ramon and his chapel had moved into the main house, to two upper rooms, so that he could be looked after. The pain was largely overcome and he improved in health and reached a kind of plateau. Earlier he had feared for a little, when he felt so ill, that he would never write anything more in his life. But now suddenly he found he could once more rise and, sitting at a table in the window, work away at his part of this book. I visited him there at that time and I was heartened to find him still so active. I began to think and hope that he might continue like this for some years to come.

Then came the surprise telephone call from Brother Raymond Christian, the Franciscan brother in the main house who, as well as looking after guests, had been responsible for those looking after Ramon. He rang one evening in mid-May. Ramon was suddenly much weaker. His blood count had changed dramatically and the doctors had tried to give him transfusions. But his blood now lacked a vital clotting agent and he kept losing more of it through the very punctures made by the needles. At last he felt so battered that he wanted them to stop trying to get blood into him and he asked just to be left in peace at the monastery. He would probably not last long. I went straight over, praying the prayer 'have mercy on *Ramon*' as I often did and wondering fearfully how much changed I would find him.

Brother Raymond Christian led me into a downstairs room and even before I had realized whose it was, I was looking at our beloved friend propped up on his pillows. He was white as they were, but otherwise completely the same as he had ever been—his face still firm and smiling delightedly, his hand reaching out to take mine, even though his arm was blue and scarred. Immediately as usual he was telling me a story of a wonderful 'sacramental' event that stood out, this time from his recent visit to the hospital.

He had been sitting in a side-ward, after the attempts to give him a transfusion, and two scars began to bleed again. He felt himself beginning to faint and slide from the chair on to the floor. He cried out for help. Two 'ministering angels', he said, came rushing to his aid and raised him up and held his wrists firmly to stop the flow. One of them was the nurse who had been looking after him already. The nurses had all become his friends and he had ministered to some of them and prayed for them as, no doubt, they prayed for him. But the other 'angel' he had not met before. She was an Indian doctor. He was struck by the beauty of her skin and her clear gaze fixed on him. At once he was talking with her of spiritual things. He found that she was a Hindu and he was able to quote to her from some of the Hindu writers he had read, such as Ramakrishnan. She was amazed and said that she had longed to find a spiritually minded Christian to talk to, but had not so far found any. He was the first! She was also impressed by his pronunciation of Indian names. He explained cheerfully that it was because of his Welsh accent of course! They laughed. Then she said gently, 'You know the truth: "All is Light, all is Life, all is Love."' 'Yes,' he said, 'I do.' This profoundly Johannine sentiment remained with him. In Christ that realization could be bound up together with our woundedness and weakness. Our struggling life and that of the whole creation were drawn up through Christ into light and life and love. Our creaturely life was transfigured and redeemed. As the Jesus Prayer flowed through him on the way back from hospital, so now he was being made one with Christ, the Light and the Life and the new Love in the Spirit!

As Ramon and I talked, Brother Raymond Christian kindly appeared with a lunch pack prepared for my return journey and quietly laid it on the bed. Ramon exclaimed, 'How posh!' teasing me for my special treatment. He too, he remarked, was also embarking on a journey now. He told me then that the night before he had had a half-dream, half-vision. 'The Lord' had approached him over a narrow and delicate bridge and, standing on it, had beckoned him to come across. 'I have come to fetch you,' he said. Ramon was full of peace and indeed excitement at this word. But he asked the Lord if he could stay a little and see myself, then, the next day, his sister, who was coming to be with him, and later Donald, his spiritual director who was also coming to say goodbye.

As he said this, I was struck again by his astonishing normality and solidity, as it were. He was alight with excitement as he spoke, but even in describing his encounter with Christ he was also his perfectly down-to-earth, humorously terrestrial self. His face, his manner, were so straightforward, as though we were chatting on a platform of a station before the train went, or a quay before he stepped aboard the boat. There was nothing unnaturally ethereal about him, despite his pallor. Indeed he remarked also that in spite of that 'vision' he was also at times very much aware of the darkness in himself and in the world. He trembled at times recollecting a saying that even right next to the very entrance into heaven there was a door that could open into the very depths of hell. He felt the chill and anxiety of that and had to hold to his Prayer. At this he grasped his black woollen prayer rope, which was round his neck. I was reminded of his describing to me earlier how he had visited Mother Agnes CSF on her deathbed (see Chapter 5). She was wearing her prayer rope in the same way. She had asked him whether it mattered if she just held the knots and said or just thought of the name of Jesus, and he had reassured her.

He told me then to take the papers that were lying in a wire basket at the foot of the bed. 'That is my half of the book,' he said. 'I hope you won't mind, but I've finished it and it's complete, just waiting for your half! You see, I was in a bit of a hurry!' he chuckled. I said how amazed and thrilled I was that he had managed it at all. He had feared that he might not. It obviously gave him great peace that he had done it. I brought that precious typescript away with me and I am working with it now as I write this.

After this, Ramon asked Brother Raymond Christian to go to his upstairs study and find a copy of one of the books he himself had written, which he had been reading again a little just now, characteristically called *Fullness of Joy*. I think that it was the last three chapters, 'Joy in life and death', 'Joy in crossing over', and 'Judgment and eternal joy' that he had been reading and that he specially wanted me to look at. He took a pen from me and wrote clearly and legibly, if a little less strongly than in previous books, on the flyleaf, the words: 'For Bishop Simon, Jean and Holly on the passing over journey. Ramon SSF Alleluia! 20 May 2000'. Then I prayed with him, speaking the Jesus Prayer aloud with him for the last time, laid hands on him and we blessed one another.

When it came to our final farewells, he seemed so extraordinarily warm, alive and normal, for all his bodily weakness, still smiling or chuckling so spontaneously, that I found myself exclaiming, 'I don't know why, but it seems so strange, somehow unbelievable, that I am saying "Goodbye" to you in this life and won't see you here any more after this!' He clasped my hand, saying, 'Well of course it is strange! Still, there it is, Simon. This is the last journey, you know.' But then almost immediately a twinkle came into his eye and his face lit up, as it often would when he was about to express some vital new thought. 'But when we get to the end of all this—there'll be...' and he raised his voice suddenly, and almost shouted, 'a Big HULLO!' And he laughed and gripped my hand. Still laughing, we parted really merrily after all. It was impossible just to be sad. I have never before nor since come away from a deathbed actually feeling exhilarated as I did then, despite the sharp sense of loss. I knew that most of all I would miss that affectionate laughter, that assurance of an ultimate 'divine comedy' in which we were all implicated.

This extraordinary capacity for joy that had always been his hall-mark prevailed for the most part in the weeks that were to follow, although it was shot through at times with inevitable darkness, moments of fear and anxiety, such as he mentioned to me during our meeting. Waiting in growing weakness and weariness, he could even begin to wonder how long the Lord was going to take to fulfil his promise to come and fetch him. But when he did slip away (on the night of 5 June 2000), there was a certainty that his essential dream/vision of Christ on the bridge had been fulfilled.

I knew that the vision of Christ first and foremost risen and ascended, but yet having borne our wounds into heaven, was central to Ramon, even as he let the stream of the Jesus Prayer flow through him. The prayer rope round his neck kept drawing him on into this awareness, even after he had been assailed by the dark.

And the secret of the marvellously firm continuity between the dying man on the bed and the genial hermit joyfully receiving us into his hut lay in his being focused on the One who, having lived to the full an earthly life with all its ups and downs and suffered and died an earthly death, is alive for ever.

This, of course, as Ramon had reminded us in that book about joy that he gave me, is true to St Francis himself, who 'died singing'. Some of Francis' brothers were taken aback when they heard singing and joy at his bedside. One of them, Brother Elias, remonstrated with him, thinking people would be scandalized. But he had, not long before, composed a further stanza welcoming Sister Death, to be added to the 'Canticle of the Sun', that extraordinary song of praise that Ramon in his book on Franciscan spirituality described as a 'fusion of the sun and the cross' given to Francis 'in the midst of suffering, darkness and blindness' (*Franciscan Spirituality*, SPCK, 1994). Francis saw in the person of the crucified and risen Christ, whose wounds he bore, the Lord of life through death, not only for himself but for the whole of humanity, the whole creation.

As I left Ramon for the last time, I knew that praying the Jesus Prayer together with him had opened up for me this whole greater perspective—the goal towards which our whole life and world are moving, which even here and now breaks in upon us through the presence of God in Christ. In him, this age and the age to come are held in one.

This was an awareness we had both received from the witness and worship of the Orthodox monastery where I had first learnt to pray the Jesus Prayer and Ramon had been greatly strengthened in praying it. The two moments in which I have recognized most strongly the New Testament emphasis on our future destiny, and on the life of the world here and now, were at Ramon's bedside and in the chapel of the monastery from which he and I had both received so much.

I was strongly reminded of this when, at Ramon's wonderful funeral in Worcester Cathedral, a group of his Franciscan brothers stood up and, almost as if it were spontaneous, burst into that glorious *Kontakion* for the dead, which I had last heard sung in the Orthodox Monastery.

I recalled then a time when I was at Coventry, when Kate, a young girl of seventeen, the lovely and lively friend of my daughter at school, for whom we had prayed so passionately at the hospital each day, died within a week of contracting meningitis. We were shattered totally and I felt quite unlike going to the Orthodox monastery where I was due to go on retreat. My whole awareness of God was blacked out. I felt suddenly quite close to despair. But mercifully I went, numb and dull as I was.

When I walked into their chapel once again, and saw the lights shining in front of the icons on the screen, the *iconostasis*, in front of me, the pictures of the saints on the walls around me, I heard once more the Jesus Prayer spoken by one voice only, first a woman's voice, then a man's, in the midst of the assembled figures of the monks and nuns standing together in the darkened space. That old sense returned to me of our lifting off together, as it were. We were all centred on the Prayer, raised up by the Spirit and reaching out to the distant light, nearer to which we seemed to move as one. And the next day at the Eucharist the interweaving voices rose and fell and the liturgy went forward with its customary majestic pace, drawing us into union with Christ, just as the Jesus Prayer had begun to do the night before. There was such a strong sense then of being taken up into the worship of heaven, through that central union with Jesus crucified, risen and exalted. Afterwards a visiting Serbian nun who had heard my news came up to me with a bunch of beeswax candles bound with a ribbon and said to me, 'Tell your daughter to light one of these each day in celebration of the new life of her friend.'

I felt convicted of having failed to be nurtured or to nurture others in this great truth of the hope in Christ of life through and beyond death. How much more we should be experiencing and exploring it in the life and worship of our churches today, 'showing forth Christ's death, till he comes'. I was able then to go back and pray with my daughter and her friends in a new way and to speak at the service of Kate, developing T.S. Eliot's injunction, 'Not farewell, fare forward, voyagers!'

That was when the rhythm of the Jesus Prayer, shared by many but spoken as one prayer, became once more the rhythm of a movement of the Spirit constantly transfiguring and transforming this world, rooted in worship and sustained by acts of love. I knew again, at the celebration of Ramon's life in the Cathedral, that whether in the world to come or in this world together we would continue to advance together from glory to glory towards our eternal goal.

CHAPTER 3

THE BIBLICAL BASIS
OF THE JESUS PRAYER

Bishop Simon writes on the Pharisee and the tax collector (Luke 18:9–14):

The Desert Fathers and Mothers

This story of the Pharisee and the tax collector was particularly popular among those men and women who went out into the desert to seek a closer walk with God in Christ in the power of the Spirit, people known as the Desert Fathers (and Mothers—there were quite a few of these, though they are more seldom mentioned!) They were the first who we know for certain used the kind of 'repeated phrase' prayers from which eventually the Jesus Prayer in its final form emerged. But they were quoting the Gospels. They loved to draw upon the Gospel stories of Jesus' saving activity. They saw themselves in the people in those stories who responded to him, especially in their desperate need and in their cries for help. We know that this particular parable from Luke, of the Pharisee and the tax collector, must have especially caught their imagination from the number of times that it is echoed or referred to. It became part of the very essence of their faith and practice, and helped to shape their profound spiritual life. Probably more than any other passage, it helped to contribute to the emergence of the Jesus Prayer as the most satisfying of all the repeated prayers.

The stories of these great people of prayer who, in succession to the martyrs, became such an inspiration to the whole Christian community, make it clear that they saw themselves as almost hopeless cases saved only by grace. They described themselves as beyond the pale, people desperately in need of divine help because they had failed morally and spiritually to be real disciples of Jesus Christ. That is why they fled into the desert to seek purification and a new beginning, to search for a fresh knowledge of God in Christ. They tried to live in a state of what John Climacus (the author of *The Ladder* already referred to on page 23) called 'joyful mourning'. This meant growth through acknowledged sin and constant repentance into trust and obedience and eventually union with Christ.

This story of the Pharisee and the tax collector gave them particular hope in that it sums up how far Jesus had turned religion inside out and upside down and opened up a way to those who might feel themselves furthest of all from God.

The Pharisee's prayer (Luke 18:9–12)

The first hearers of the parable would have been quite shocked and amazed by it. The Pharisee was the ideal faithful and obedient Jew. By his fervent adherence to the Law, he seemed to stand at the very centre of a renewed and righteous Israel or 'people of God'. His struggle for meticulous moral probity, his quest for the utmost honesty and just dealing towards all, his sexual purity and his intensely disciplined religious observance made him a model for his society. He stood out, it seemed, most impressively and enviably from the great mass of moderately sensual, frequently dishonest, fairly selfish and plausible worldlings, those who, in the Pharisee's prayer in the parable, are called 'the rest of humanity' (Luke 18:11). He saw himself as standing at the summit of a reformed institutional religion. But here the danger of his developing an unconscious complacency, and of his implicit contempt for others, is drastically highlighted.

The tax collector's prayer (Luke 18:13–14)

The tax collector, on the other hand, was about the most excluded person, the most shut out from God and from decent human community, that it was possible to find. He was part of the marginal riff-raff, on the edge of his world, compensating by his wealth and a certain shabby kind of power and manipulativeness for the extent to which the best people in his society would despise him. He was perhaps drifting into further worldly indulgence the more he became alienated from the very kind of goodness and fulfilment for which something within him craved. He was part of a shadowy underworld in the poorer parts of which lurked prostitutes, criminals and informers. A surprise visit to the Temple drew out of him a poignant cry, 'God, *hilastheti* ('expiate', the word here translated in verse 13 as 'be merciful': that is, 'make atonement' for me, a sinner—literally 'the sinner'). But this was a request too unlikely, he might have felt, for a just God even to be able to grant. How could it be done? It was a plea that arose from a greater exile and loneliness than any mere collection of single transgressions could have brought about. Such a sinner was not just someone guilty of a large number of particular moral lapses. This prayer was that from a person guilty of a heap of sins ranging from mere peccadiloes even to major crimes. It was the desperate appeal of someone totally outcast, cut off from God, from his whole spiritual heritage and roots, a stranger to the promises offered to the rest of his people. By his very job, co-operating with the hated Romans and thus exploiting his own people, he had made himself of all human beings the most profoundly, socially and spiritually isolated and alone.

How *could* such a person be 'justified', made righteous, and brought through into a complete relationship with God and with all humankind? It would need nothing short of a miracle. But Jesus points to the real significance of the utter humility, honesty and naked faith of his prayer. It is a prayer for the opening up of a new possibility.

Jesus and the Kingdom community

Jesus came into the scene as one in whom God was ready to bring in that new possibility. Among the many varieties of Jewish belief at that time, there was a widespread expectation of a spiritual leader called the Messiah, a word meaning in Hebrew 'the anointed one', divinely empowered to usher in a final age, the reign or kingdom of God. He was to become the centre and nucleus of a new Israel, and the vehicle of a new, immediately direct and total presence of the living God, indwelling his people by his Spirit—'God in Strength', as it has been called.[2] The word 'Messiah' or 'the Lord's Anointed' was translated into Greek as *Christos*, with its overtones in the Roman empire of a universal ruler. The Christ would come to usher in the sovereign sway of God's will running through all things. This is what Jesus called 'the Kingdom of God'. For those who entrusted themselves to him in his lifetime, and even more after his death and resurrection, he already indeed embodied that Kingdom. He was seen as *Christos Autobasileia*, that is, the Anointed One who is the Kingdom-in-Himself. And he came to inaugurate that Kingdom by inviting all those in and around the old Israel into the new Kingdom community, the ultimate fulfilment of the promises to Moses and to the prophets of old. Once this re-creative work of his was initiated, then all the 'nations', the 'Gentiles', all humankind, would be drawn in.

Jesus began this great initiative of God by calling everyone into what was to be the nucleus of a truly renewed Israel. From the outset it was open to all who would respond to the opportunity of an intimate and transforming relationship with God, starting at once. All varieties of people could come and be changed into the new people of God, the Israel of the end time, as they became joined to Jesus and to each other in a new self-giving love, to which a special name was given in the Greek of the New Testament—*agape*. Another Greek word that Jesus uses to invite his hearers into this way of the Kingdom community is 'turn (change direction) and keep turning'—in New Testament Greek *metanoiete* (*meta* meaning 'beyond' and *nous* meaning 'mind'), which seems to imply changing your whole mindset, letting his invitation 'blow your mind'! English versions have translated this word as 'repent', but essentially it means 'turn'—turn into the new way of the Kingdom community as you follow Jesus.

Former tax collectors, prostitutes, poor people as well as some rich, women as well as men responded. So indeed did former Pharisees and former Sadducees (the ruling religious establishment —these last, like the rich, found it much harder to receive the invitation). The sick, the suffering and the damaged in mind or body, they all poured in. Luke's Gospel especially emphasizes the place in the Kingdom for the oppressed, the sick, the women and the poor. Only one thing mattered, as this parable makes clear— that total, reckless turning to God in utter self-humbling and trust, as expressed in the tax collector's prayer. You must be ready 'to lose your life to find it' and be cast into the arms of God the loving parent, whom Jesus enacted and embodied. Then you will become part of this marvellous, inclusive gathering in, this fellowship of the unlike. You will be drawn into what is, in truth, to be nothing less than a new beginning for the whole of creation. The tax collector in Jesus' parable represents all those outsiders like him—a Zacchaeus or a Levi, the guests at the feasts Jesus went to so readily—who through Jesus' preaching poured into the Kingdom.

But this new creation could not be completed until the forces of destruction always at work in the world assailed it, using the hardened resistance of those in power in the old Israel and in the Gentile world, the Romans. Jesus had to see the whole delicate venture stopped and smashed and scattered. Even those at the core of the attempt to shape a new people of God, 'the Twelve', his disciples, failed and fled. Now it was clear that he alone must first take on himself the destiny, the tragic fate of his people, upon whom had become concentrated the fatal flaw, the universal evil of human-kind. On behalf of all, Jesus, the one true and faithful representative of Israel and of humanity as God meant it to be, must die. The old (dis-)order must be destroyed. At the heart of creation, there must be a breaking and a remaking.

So came the resurrection, the fulfilment of many dreams, myths and legends of death and rebirth through the ages. The possibility of a new life dawned. The goal of the Kingdom, a state of harmony and all-enfolding peace and justice, described in the Jewish word *shalom*, opened up. The prayer of the tax collector in Jesus' parable is finally answered. The only way forward now is the way of repentance (or turning) and forgiveness 'preached in his name to all nations' (Luke 24:47), enabling continuous *metanoia*, continuous turning to the risen Christ, and thus to the God to whom he has given us access. This is made possible after his resurrection by the release of a new power to turn, a new energy, the Spirit of God, increasingly described as the Holy Spirit.

Through the outpouring of that Spirit, symbolized by fire and light, and indeed by immersion or baptism in water, union with Christ was given to many, and the new people of God was formed, the fellowship of the unlike in which the equivalents of the tax collector would find their joyful place. The rhythm of a continuous renewal of life, continuous turning to Christ, within that union is expressed not only in the breaking of bread and sharing of wine together, but in prayer. Through the shaping Spirit, the Jesus Prayer emerges as a prayer of that ongoing renewal and growth into union with Christ among those who work to prepare the way for the coming of the Kingdom.

The Jesus Prayer takes the prayer of the tax collector up into the life of the new Israel, in which he, and all those who cry out with him to God, find a homecoming. He is the reminder to us, as to the Desert Fathers and Mothers of old, that Jesus Christ has brought God to those who feel cut off from God, people of all cultures, of all religions and of none. Jesus, as none other, is God for the ungodly. In the strength of the 'Spirit of Jesus', as the Holy Spirit is some-times called in the New Testament, the Jesus Prayer is always the prayer for those who cannot otherwise pray.

However far people may feel themselves to be from whatever God or gods they have heard about, Jesus can be for them the assurance of 'God with us'. However little they know how or what to pray, the Jesus Prayer can offer an immediate way of praying and of finding and being found by the presence of Christ. Then, as the Spirit prays the Prayer within them, they will find themselves being brought home through Christ into the arms of the One whom he called 'Abba' (intimate loving parent and friend). So in union with all who pray this Prayer, we can be made one with the love and light and life of the eternal triune God.

Brother Ramon writes on blind Bartimaeus (Luke 18:35–43):

Universal yearning

These are two very different men presenting themselves before God in these passages from Luke 18. Whatever may be true of the tax collector in his loneliness, awareness of guilt and unworthy longing for reconciling love, he certainly stands alone, without friends, intercessors or loved ones. He is a symbol of human yearning and seems to be longing for something never known before.

As for blind Bartimaeus, he sits wearily begging at the roadside. Though his eyes cannot see, they can certainly weep. He cries out in anguish, 'Lord, let me see *again*.' That 'again' means that he once could see: he was not born blind. Something had happened, some catastrophe, accident, act of violence, period of neglect or disease that had reduced him suddenly, or over a long period, into the dark and empty world that he now knew in his lonely begging, sitting in the dust at Jericho.

He is a symbol of the human yearning that somehow knows that God has made us for himself, and that our hearts are restless until they find rest in him. And simply because of the fact of that yearning, there is a faint hope kindled from time to time in his imagination, in his prayers, in the moments of strange stirring in the depths of his spirit. That is the mystic stirring of the Holy Spirit who is universally present and active. So it is that in such a situation, he is placed at his usual spot at the Jericho roadside for another bleak and empty day of begging to keep body and soul together.

He had been there some hours when he became conscious of some movement among the people. Groups were gathering, murmuring excitedly, conversing with an expectant attitude. 'What's going on?' he asked. 'Is something important happening, someone important coming this way?'

'Yes,' replied those who could be bothered to answer. 'Jesus of Nazareth is passing by.'

Bartimaeus seems not to have met Jesus previously, and he could not chase after him, having no eyes to guide him. But perhaps he had heard of him, dreamed of him, perhaps imagined this moment when such an episode could take place when his need would call upon Christ, healer and saviour—and Bartimaeus would see again.

There was no doubt what he *should* do—the only thing he *could* do—and that was to cry out in desperate need. The only way a man or woman can cry out from such depths is from despair or wonder. And it is from despair, not unmingled with wonder, that Bartimaeus began to cry:

> *Jesus, Son of God, have mercy on me!*
> *Jesus, Son of God, have mercy on me!*
> *Jesus, Son of God, have mercy on me!*

Persistence and repetition were absolutely essential, and they reveal the determination and seriousness of Bartimaeus' situation. It was now or never. Jesus was approaching. He was passing by! But the cry had to rise above the murmuring of the crowd, the idle curiosity of the people. It is impossible not to hear the constant repetition of these ancient words from all parts of the Church of God, chanted, sung and shouted through the ages:

Kyrie eleison! Lord, have mercy!
Kyrie eleison! Lord, have mercy!
Kyrie eleison! Lord, have mercy!

So Jesus approached, and as he came near he was aware of the cry that arose both above the murmur of the crowd and above the noise of the ecclesiastical leaders who lined the way. For the leaders, it was a matter of religious interest, controversy and dogmatic rectitude. For the crowd, it was 'What is going on today?' and the use of their eyes, ears, tongues, hands and feet to get into the midst of this new teaching and person of Jesus. Of what value were Bartimaeus' eyes in such a context? Well, to Bartimaeus, everything! For him, only one thing was necessary, and that was to get the full and concentrated attention of Jesus the healer and wonder worker. It was clear to his inward soul that Jesus acted out of compassion and pity, hence the word *eleison* ('have mercy'). So the text makes it clear: 'He shouted even more loudly' (Luke 18:39).

And then there came to his keenly listening ears (there was nothing wrong with them!) the blessed words: 'What do you want me to do for you?' He replied, 'Lord, let me see again' (Luke 18:41). There it was—a simple plea that contained in itself all the yearning of his heart, and symbolized the universal human quest for light, salvation, healing, forgiveness and restoration. He pitches it at the level of simple, physical need, but we can see in it a whole cosmos, fallen, alienated, disillusioned and longing for what it once had, for what it could have, for what it would have—if God was merciful and gracious.

Does the Jesus Prayer promise all this? Well, I believe it does. Since the 1970s, when I began to learn more of it from Eastern Orthodoxy, and found myself more deeply grounded in the biblical tradition of the power of the name of Jesus, it has become increasingly clear that the personal leads through the corporate, through to the cosmic and universal. Participation in the Jesus Prayer is ultimately felt to be a means of entry into the very life of God, leading to our being made 'partakers of the divine nature' (2 Peter 1:4). More will be said about this vision in the last chapter. And we will thereby have a share in the ultimate transfiguration of the world in the glory of the second advent of Christ.

In the case of blind Bartimaeus, we hear the words that Jesus speaks by the authority of God and the power of the Holy Spirit: 'Receive your sight; your faith has saved you' (Luke 18:42). The result was spontaneous and widespread, for not only did Bartimaeus receive his sight, following Jesus as saviour and healer, but the effect on all around caused the people to glorify God. And there were even religious leaders among them, for nothing is too hard for God!

These two passages that Bishop Simon and I have reflected upon bring us right into the centre of the repetition of the Jesus Prayer. I certainly feel my identification with the sinful tax collector and with blind Bartimaeus as I say with penitence and wonder: 'Lord Jesus Christ, Son of God, have mercy on me, a sinner.'

CHAPTER 4

LEARNING TO PRAY THE JESUS PRAYER ON A RETREAT

Bishop Simon writes:

When I first went on an eight-day retreat, based on the Exercises of St Ignatius with a Jesuit guide, I was impressed by one complete difference between that and any other retreat or quiet day that I had been involved in before. This retreat was totally focused on drawing closer to Jesus Christ, seeking indeed to be drawn into union with him through meditating on the Bible, on the Exercises and on prayer (and daily communion). The main activity of the day was not listening to talks, nor toying with a book or two and feeling vaguely edified. The main work was the sheer attempt to pray. On the first day I found myself to be virtually a spiritual bankrupt.

My retreat guide had seen me at the start and set me on my way, agreeing with me on my aim and then telling me to go and pray for three hours at least during the day at different times. I found that my mind wandered and thoughts flew everywhere except to God. The next morning, after a restless night, I went to my guide to tell him that I had got nowhere and that, sadly, I probably now needed to abandon the attempt. He listened sympathetically. Then he commented, half to himself as it seemed, 'Yes, yes! That's what they all say to begin with. Now today I want you to make it four hours. In the middle, why not go for a walk?' He then pointed to the meditation I was to do and told me to get on with it. It went a little better that day.

That day, the figure of Jesus really stood out from the Gospel scene I was trying to envisage, in the usual Ignatian way. But the background faded away. The thoughts I had had slipped into oblivion and while I was still wide awake I found myself no longer 'envisaging' anything or anyone but simply entering into the presence of Jesus without sound or sight as I let the flow of the Jesus Prayer carry me forward. Eventually, as the desire to spend more time doing this grew, I found myself constantly turning back from my wandering thoughts. At the end of each time of prayer, I found I could make each one of the acts of commitment to which Ignatius' words and pictures were pointing. By the end of the week I was gripped and felt sad to be tearing myself away.

From this I learnt a vital point. A good retreat is one that makes you spend the time, above all else, struggling to pray, seeking the presence of Christ without giving up. The retreat 'conductor' is only there to offer background support. Your central task is to grow towards a deeper union with God in Christ through the leading of the Spirit. Even if it is a retreat that includes listening to talks, these should only be, like the conversations I had had with my 'guide', an aid to the central activity, the prayer of each participant.

So I resolved that in any retreat I conducted I would direct my talks primarily to facilitating the growth in prayer of each participant. I would also encourage every one of those who attended to come and have a talk with me so that the Holy Spirit could use this to give them each some particular personal help in their contribution to our central task. I make this emphasis into the substance of my introductory talk at any retreat that I lead on the Jesus Prayer.

Any particular method of prayer is only a means to that central task. The retreat is not to 'promote' the Jesus Prayer but to *offer* it to people as one useful way of entering into communion with God in Christ. That is the focus. The reason why Ramon and I and anyone else feel ready to commend this apparently simple and universal method of prayer is that, as one of the most ancient Christian traditions, it has been a proven method of helping people to come into this communion with Christ. The power of the name reverently invoked in the Spirit can bring us to him. Each act of saying the Prayer gives us a fresh opportunity of turning to him, away from our self-concern and the distractions that divert us.

To say the words with our voice or in our heart, 'Lord Jesus Christ, Son of God', is to return again and again to the One who is our centre and source and goal. On the consistent stream of the Prayer, our mind and heart can keep being borne into the enfolding embrace of his love. Many guides to this way of praying who have written about it through the centuries, especially Bishop Theophan the Recluse (1815–94)[3], in the Russian flowering of the Jesus Prayer in the 19th century, have emphasized what he in particular described as praying 'with the mind in the heart'. We must seek to let the thinking, speaking part of us 'go down', as he put it, 'into the heart'—that is, into the feeling, desiring and also willing part of us, the place from which our longings and aspirations chiefly arise. We ask God the Holy Spirit to enable us increasingly to fuse together our thought and our will, our reason and our emotions, until our whole being reaches out to find (and to be found by) the presence of God in Jesus Christ. We usually start by 'wanting to want' that presence. The words we speak or frame in our minds will then gradually draw the rest of us round into the direction towards which we know we must seek to move, as a punt is gradually drawn round by the movement of the pole.

As we start to go with the movement of the flow of the Spirit, we can of course let the stream of the Prayer flow into and through and beyond any other modes of praying that we may be led to use.

I encourage people to use the prayer rope that those who taught me helped me to use, supreme among them Archimandrite Sophrony and his fellow monks and nuns in the monastery he founded of St John the Baptist, Tolleshunt Knights, in Essex. Brother Ramon also encouraged me greatly in this, as I have mentioned above. The rope has a wooden bead placed on it, at the end of every twenty knots in the hundred that make up the whole cord. As you hold each knot between forefinger and thumb, you say the Jesus Prayer once, and then you pass on to the next knot and say it again, and so on. When you come to a wooden bead, you can pause for a time on it, and make use of it for a different purpose. I learnt to start praying this Prayer by taking hold of the tassel, which can be seen as a symbol of Pentecost, the outpouring of the Spirit, and then asking the Holy Spirit to pray within me. Next, holding the first large bead underneath and the threefold knot above, I asked that Christ, being lifted up on the cross, might draw me to himself and through himself into the communion of the Trinity. After that, with the first ordinary knot, I was launched into the Jesus Prayer.

With the next bead that comes along, I sometimes, if so led, pause to have a kind of conversation with the Lord, clearing away any particular distracting burden of sin or need or concern that may be hindering me, and entrusting all to him. When the second bead comes along, I may—only if it seems right and not as a kind of rule—pause to mention some particular person or situation that seems laid upon me. Sometimes, if that is very strong, I can put the name of the person or group in mind in the place of 'me, a sinner' for the next series of knots, although that is not strictly necessary. After all, when we pray 'have mercy on *me*', we are praying for ourselves as one tiny part, representing the whole, the human family and indeed the entire creation.

On the next bead and indeed any of the others, we may want just to be totally wordless for a time, as a bird flying sometimes pauses with wings outstretched and floats along a current of air. We may want to listen also, in case we hear in our hearts something being said to us, until the moment comes to move the wings again as we resume, 'with the mind in our heart', the saying of the Jesus Prayer. But then, as the Prayer carries us on the next time round, so to speak, further and further into the stillness of the presence, we may well end with a time of silence, as Ramon and I did when we prayed together.

From the time of the Desert Fathers onwards, some have used the prayer as a way into a profound *hesychia* (stillness), and have found that as the Prayer streams on within them, silence is given with it. Indeed, they have spoken of times when even the Prayer ceased. Some have clearly seen the Prayer itself as a kind of silence of mind and heart, words that in themselves are no longer separate from silence, but rather hold the praying person in the stillness of the presence, the divine *shalom*, the peace of God. I nearly always end up the saying of the Prayer with the words of the first part of it, 'Lord Jesus Christ, Son of God', ending where I began, 'in the presence'.

Homecoming

Our whole understanding of prayer and of how to pray must always, then, be subordinate to our prime intention of openness to the presence of the person of Christ. Through the Spirit's work within and among us, we can call upon Jesus by name. So we can start by asking the Spirit, before all else, to open up for us the union with Jesus Christ that is open to us through our baptism, and that can begin to be realized just as soon as we acknowledge him as Lord and surrender our life into his hands.

When we turn to 'God with us' or, as the promise in the Baptism service puts it, 'turn to Christ', through calling upon him as Lord, we can experience the first moment of all prayer in his name, the opening up to us of his welcoming and loving and healing presence. He comes to us as he came to his disciples in the upper room when they were huddled together in despair and guilt for their failure, with the doors shut for fear (John 20:19–23), and had come to the end of themselves. And his first words were not of recrimination but of welcome and acceptance. He said to them, 'Peace [*shalom* peace, enfolding heaven and earth, all humankind and each human heart] be with you.'

This is the joy of our first and final arrival in our true home. It is the joy of homecoming. I spoke of my first visit at Brother Ramon's hermitage as being such a homecoming. There are certain places that almost all of us have known, where to step over the threshold is to step into our true place.

So I often quote Gerard Manley Hopkins' poem 'In the Valley of the Elwy':

> I remember a house where all were good
> To me, God knows, deserving no such thing:
> Comforting smell breathed at very entering,
> Fetched fresh, as I suppose, off some sweet wood.

I always imagine that that sweet wood might well be the wood of the cross, of a welcome which is profoundly forgiving and restoring. Here we can dwell in his love.

> That cordial air made those kind people a hood
> All over, as a bevy of eggs the mothering wing
> Will, or mild nights the new morsels of Spring:
> Why, it seemed of course; seemed of right it should.

This is what newcomers to a genuinely Christian community can feel upon entering. I have experienced it at places like Lee Abbey, stepping through the familiar doors and into the Octagonal Lounge where a log fire is burning, gazing down on that unforgettable view of the curve of the little bay, with the glimpse of the infinite ocean beyond and the great cliff with its tangled woods sweeping down beyond—and then being met by young members of the community who seem so relaxed and welcoming. Or again, recently, when my wife, Jean, and I visited the Darvell Bruderhof community in Sussex. Here is a large company of people of all kinds of professions and backgrounds, social classes and nationalities, made up of many families, and of the old and the young, at all ages and stages, sharing everything in common and committed to peace-making, to justice and to living and proclaiming the way of life described in the Sermon on the Mount. We spent the afternoon and evening with them, hearing about their life, seeing their varied activities and being entertained by a whole range of people. In the evening, we walked round to their farm, through the country near at hand and then visiting their burial ground, which was an attractive garden, a place of peace and beauty where we sat on a bench among the trees for a while, talking contentedly with the family, parents and their children, who were looking after us. The atmosphere of the whole settlement was so exhilarating that we were reluctant to leave, feeling that we had felt the touch of what C.S. Lewis would have called 'a breath of air from a far country'. We wanted to keep recalling it.

It is striking how often it happens that a loving couple, when they first fall for each other, find that each sees in the other all that person's gift and promise, and each feels their own real nature and destiny miraculously affirmed. Later it might seem to have been an illusion. But it actually contains a great deal of truth. It suggests the potential that each of the two and, above all, their relationship with each other could hold. There may be a long way to go. But they would do well never to forget what they first saw in each other, and what each helped the other to feel about themselves. They need to keep renewing that vision.

This kind of homecoming and recognition should be the beginning of prayer. The first move in prayer through Christ is to recall how you are loved and forgiven. Paul's great prayers in the epistles always begin with this kind of thanksgiving for all that we have received in Christ. He is always urging that we should 'become what we are' and what we were made to be and can now become. We have to start from that. Life with Christ and prayer with Christ are both a journey that begins with homecoming and arrival. It is a story that begins at the end. Our self-generated lives run out of energy. We find ourselves at the beginning of a new life, which rises out of that end of ourselves which in Christ is our true beginning!

Watchman Nee, in his commentary on Ephesians, *Sit, Walk, Stand* (Kingsway Communications, 1972), rightly emphasized how, through its opening prayer, Paul's letter begins with 'our being raised up with Christ to sit with him in heavenly places' (Ephesians 2:6). Nee then leads us on into walking with Christ, and finally standing with him, armed by our confidence in being so much loved, to resist all that is spiritually opposed to his purpose.

So our prayer should start from realizing his great love for us, and only then seeking to entrust ourselves and all else to that love. The words 'Lord Jesus Christ, Son of God...' (or sometimes I say, to bring the truth home to me, 'Love of God...') should always be enabling us to rest in that still presence before anything more at all, as we seek with the whole creation of which we are a tiny part to come home to him.

It is only as we really know ourselves to be loved and valued by the living God that we can be given the courage to change, to grow more and more into the people we were meant to be. It is only in the security of that love that we will be freed to give ourselves more and more to the needs of others and to the transformation of our world.

Journeying

But if Jesus' first appearances to his disciples after his resurrection offered them, and all who would come after them, a homecoming, he did leave it at that. John's Gospel, of course, gives us the whole episode in a few sentences. But it must have taken longer. Jesus the Christ comes among them (John 20:19–23) and says to them, 'Peace be with you', showing them his hands and his side as signs of the way in which he has overcome all that had resisted God's purpose in him, both in the disciples and in the world. He shows them that the new love he came to release among us is invincible now, and they, as they see him, perhaps through their tears, are indeed brought home to their true destiny and purpose. All sending out, all mission in his name, will have to keep springing from this vision.

Then Jesus confirms their joy and their knowledge of his great love for each of them, as for each of us. He breathes on them his Holy Spirit, and his love is poured out in their hearts. This is the bridge between the first movement of his love and the second. For he goes on to recommission them to be his agents in the world, drawing people into his 'Way', preparing the way for his final appearing and for the homecoming of all.

This is also the sequence we shall always experience as we begin to enter into communion with him. First, we receive his forgiveness and love, the outpouring of that *agape* love into us and among us as we entrust ourselves anew to him. That should always be the first movement in prayer, as it seems to be in the prayers we find in the New Testament. In the Jesus Prayer it comes with the words, 'Lord Jesus Christ' as we are brought into his presence. But the second movement springs out of the first. The knowledge of his love realized deep within us now enables us to seek both to bring about change in ourselves and to bring that change to others and ultimately to everything. This, surely, is what the words 'have mercy upon us, have mercy upon me, a sinner!' truly express. We find welling up within us a heartfelt yearning, a real longing to be different from how we have been and to become what we truly are. This becomes also a longing for our whole world to be similarly transformed. Such a longing is accompanied by sharp insights into the way we have failed and a strong confidence in the way we can reach out again for the wholeness and the fulfilment that we know is our destiny. It is both a painful and a joyful moment. It is a longing that is to be turned into a struggle to fulfil that longing.

You know how it is when you become aware of being profoundly loved and valued and affirmed by someone you respect and love. You now want to be different and you know that you can begin to be. You can at least 'fail towards' your new goal! That is, you can reach out to grasp and be grasped by it, even though you know you can never fully attain it. That is part of the repeated prayer, 'Have mercy upon us!' Enfold us in your love, draw us to yourself, use us to serve your purpose of love in your creation!

So the yearning becomes a journeying in hope. But this is not just to happen within the microcosm of our divided and confused self. The change we are looking for in the little world of our heart is to take place also in the macrocosm of the world around us—our human society, local, national and international; the natural world; the animal world; our threatened environment. If the darkness and brokenness of our hearts can be healed and brought into union with the whole redemptive process inaugurated on Christ's cross, so can the darkness and brokenness of the wider world. There also we must be made God's instruments through our intercession and action.

Prayer, as a part of the whole relationship with God in Christ that it sustains, thus always moves from homecoming to journeying. It moves from rejoicing at being brought into the love of God and from dwelling ever more deeply in that love, to yearning for wholeness of myself and for all; from repentance (turning) and painful yet joyful growth in love, to intercession and practical service.

'Still and still moving...'

When I lead a retreat, on the last evening I invite everybody to come together in the chapel. We then embark on a corporate participation in the Jesus Prayer. I have usually led this, and the others, as in the monastery, join in silently, not speaking but yet following the prayer 'with the mind in the heart'. We are focusing on the presence and person of Jesus, crucified and risen, and with us always 'even to the end of time' (Matthew 28:20). We seek together to leave all other mental activity behind and simply to be still in the presence. As we will already have experienced, this inevitably becomes, so to speak, a symphony with two movements—of rejoicing in the presence of Jesus Christ, and, as we address him as Son of God, being led into the presence of God as the loving parent ('Abba') to whom the Son brings us as the Holy Spirit prays within us. We become conscious of the Trinity. In the divine light and love, we surrender ourselves wholly to the Three-in-One in wordless adoration and praise. But then, we are almost bound, sooner or later, to be filled with longing for the stilling and reordering of the chaos in the microcosm of our own hearts and in the macrocosm of our society. We long for the whole tortured creation to be healed and made new. The Jesus Prayer encapsulates this double movement and finds in Christ the One who holds both parts together—the joy and the yearning, the contemplation and the intercession.

As together we invoke his name, the Jesus Prayer quite naturally becomes a fusion of contemplation and intercession. Perhaps there is no other mode of contemplative prayer which to the same extent combines an entry into total stillness (*hesychia*) before the Lord with an infinite yearning for the world. The Spirit prays here within us with groanings that cannot be uttered, entering into our own groanings for ourselves and into the groaning of the whole creation. And yet this groaning is held within a vast joy, a worship and adoration of heaven glimpsed and participated in through and beyond the clouds, as in the Revelation of John (ch. 4; 7:9–17; 14:1–5; 15:2–4; all leading on to ch. 21).

Here once again the Jesus Prayer is only a simple means, simple as the simplest petitionary prayers in the Gospels, a means by which, as the Desert Fathers showed us, we can be drawn into the mystery of Christ's incarnation and Passion. It is only in and through him that the fusion of contemplation and intercession is brought into being. The Jesus Prayer becomes a reflection, a reverberation of his true nature, as one in whom earth is drawn into heaven, time into its eternal goal.

In the letter to the Hebrews, we are given the picture of Jesus as one who *both* has completed the work of our transformation and sits at the right hand of God (Hebrews 1:3; 10:12–13) *and yet* 'ever lives to make intercession for us' (Hebrews 7:25; compare 4:13–16). John describes him as 'our Advocate in heaven' (1 John 2:1). Jesus carries our wounds into heaven, and his very presence with the Father is a continuing plea for us. It is out of this fusion of triumph and continuing struggle that the French artist, Georges Rouault, could write underneath one of his great portrayals of the suffering Christ in his sequence of etchings called 'Miserere' (1916–18), 'He will suffer until the end of the world.' Yet even in these works Rouault still conveyed something of the implicit majesty and sovereignty of the Christ of the San Damiano crucifix in Ramon's chapel. The ultimate truth is one of serene joy overarching the struggle. The 'Yes' is greater than the 'No' and contains it (2 Corinthians 1:29). The great intercessors in Christ, through their pain, radiate this Eastern Christian joy and affirmation just as, in the West, Mother Julian gazing upon and through the agony of Christ crucified saw the Trinity in majesty. While she entered intensely into the sufferings of the Passion, yet she declared unequivocally that 'all shall be well'.

Jesus is the one point in the whole universe at which the triune God can be seen to hold together both homecoming and journeying, setting the journey itself within that arrival out of which it proceeds and in which it finds its consummation. In him and in prayer in his name, we can learn to be, in T.S. Eliot's familiar phrase, 'still and still moving' (from the end of 'East Coker' in the *Four Quartets*, and prefigured in 'Burnt Norton' in the description of 'a Chinese jar' that 'moves perpetually in its stillness'). We can learn to worship and to adore and to rejoice with joy inexpressible, and yet within that very worship to yearn and to long and to struggle with the journeying creation. In Christ we learn to see that God himself reigns and yet journeys with us.

Epilogue: 'dwell in me and I in you'

This is the place at which all the Jesus Prayer retreats that I have made and all those that I have conducted have their climax. There are always the three movements in each retreat. The first is 'Homecoming', the second 'Journeying' and the third that I have simply called 'Still and Still Moving'. Indeed that could be the title for the whole retreat. When I can, however, I end with a fourth session entitled 'Dwell in me, and I in you' (John 15:4). It is about the practice of the Jesus Prayer as a growing indwelling in Jesus Christ and, through him, in the Father through the Spirit. At this point I look at how we go beyond all thoughts or meanings simply into a silence in which all is gathered into one, as all the colours of the rainbow can merge into pure light.

At the end of the corporate time in the chapel, we have sometimes found ourselves led into staying together for a profound and total silence in which people remain present for as long or as short a time as they feel led to do. This has become a supremely valuable moment. We recognize that something of this silence is present in every saying of the Jesus Prayer, alone or together. (It is always truly a corporate prayer, though it has relatively rarely in its history been said corporately as I experienced it in the monastery.)

This final silence, however, brings out the point that the retreat talks, like the icons in the chapel, simply create the setting. They point to something of the meaning of practising the presence of Christ in such a prayer. But we can also pray the Prayer apart from all but the most generalized consciousness of the three moments I have presented—'homecoming', 'journeying' and their integration in 'still and still moving'. We can simply cling to the bare trust that we shall be held 'in Christ'. We can let all thoughts and images drop away. In the silence, we are reshaped like the caterpillar in the chrysalis hanging there within its darkness. Only thus can we share in the reshaping of the creation itself. We can at least begin to explore through this way of prayer, and discover that as it becomes nearer to being the way of Christ, we can sometimes catch a glimpse of what it might mean to die to the old self and rise to the new.

CHAPTER 5

THE SIMPLICITY AND PROFUNDITY
OF THE JESUS PRAYER

Brother Ramon writes:

This chapter is pragmatic—'how to do it' spelled out. But it will also reflect how simple yet how profound is the Prayer in its usage among both beginners and mature believers. Here is its simplicity: 'Lord Jesus Christ, Son of God, have mercy on me, a sinner.' And yet Bishop Simon and I, for over twenty years, have been traversing, exploring, investigating and being moved, stirred and transfigured by its profound depth and power. Let me give you a couple of illustrations.

Some years before I began my hermit exploration, I participated in a 'monastic day' at a Methodist junior school near Canterbury. The children loved it, and I am persuaded they look back to it as a day to remember—a milestone in their childhood experience.

The boys and girls had made their homespun habits out of towels, scraps and odd pieces, consisting of a basic robe garment with rope or belt and 'capuce' or hood. Every pupil was involved in some kind of work that would have monastic overtones—some of it specifically so, like calligraphy, psalmody, chapel offices and religious painting and writing, and some of it stemming from the tradition, like garden-ing, cooking, first-aid teaching and visiting the sick.

My task was to visit the various groups in my Franciscan habit, and to lead them all in a teaching session of the Jesus Prayer. I took along my giant icon of Rublev's *Trinity*, as well as my prayer rope with its 100 knots and prayer stool. About 200 of us gathered in the chapel, and after some simple and basic words of explanation and a learning of the brief Prayer, we launched into our rhythmic repetition and a period of silence. They had never done anything like that before, and realized that they did not need the habits, icon, candle, rope or prayer stool, but simply the words from a sincere heart, repeated in silence, walking or fellowship—simplicity itself.

The second illustration comes from when I took holy communion to Mother Agnes CSF at our convent in Compton Durville, and she asked me if I would teach her how to say the Jesus Prayer. This was shortly before her death and she was not capable of anything but direct simplicity. So I took her a prayer rope and taught her to finger it, saying the words of the prayer simply and directly to our Lord within her heart.

When I returned a month later, I found her wearing the cord around her neck. She said, 'Brother, I cannot remember all the words, so I just go around the rope and repeat the name of Jesus. Is that all right?' Of course it was all right.

In terms of the Jesus Prayer's profundity, I remember one morning when I was visiting Tolleshunt Knights Orthodox monastery, when I joined with the fathers, sisters and lay people at their session of the Jesus Prayer in their chapel. The bishop from Romania repeated the prayer in French and English, and we joined in whatever way we felt appropriate. The wisdom and ancient holiness of Orthodoxy pervaded the atmosphere, saturating me in profound and exquisite yearning. This was the stuff of holiness.

Definition and explanation

I could leave it there and allow the Spirit to take you deeper, but that is exactly what this book is meant to do under the same Spirit, so at this point we shall describe the Prayer and the way of practising it on a regular basis.

The power of the name of God is abundantly clear in the Old Testament (consider Jacob's encounter with the name of Yahweh in his dream in Genesis 28:10–13 and his wrestling with God in Genesis 32:23–32). The whole of the New Testament resounds with the revelation of the saving name of Jesus.

As Bishop Simon has told, the post-biblical origins of the Jesus Prayer are found in the deserts of Palestine, Egypt and Syria where the Desert Fathers and Mothers lived in simplicity, austerity and prayer. Such lives were a witness to the saving gospel and as a testimony against the developing worldliness of the Constantinian Church.

The Jesus Prayer has remained part of the praying of both clergy and laity in the Orthodox tradition down the centuries. You can imagine the wonder of being handed a prayer rope as a novice on Mount Athos, beginning a whole pilgrimage of simplicity and profundity, being caught up in this way of praying. This is not the whole of prayer, of course, and practitioners in both East and West will insist on the accompanying grounding and fellowship within the liturgical and eucharistic life of the Church of God.

Repetition

Jesus said, 'When you are praying, do not heap up empty phrases as the Gentiles do; for they think that they will be heard because of their many words... Your Father knows what you need before you ask him' (Matthew 6:7–8). He speaks here against the 'ledger mentality' which is the basic attitude of pharisaic religion. Repetition is important in the saying of the Jesus Prayer, but it is biblical and not 'vain' repetition—there is a stark difference!

The Jesus Prayer acknowledges the divine mercy, the free grace of God by which alone salvation is to be received, and Jesus took note of the words of Isaiah: 'This people honours me with their lips, but their hearts are far from me; in vain do they worship me, teaching human precepts as doctrines' (Matthew 15:8–9; Isaiah 29:13).

It is *vain* repetition against which Jesus speaks, wordy multi-plication, empty religiosity. But the repetition of repentance and adoration is of another order, as we saw in the repetition of blind Bartimaeus, which brought him healing and salvation. Such repet-ition, together with the opening repeated *Kyries* of the Eucharist, indicates the heartfelt cries of wonder that call down the divine compassion. Indeed, they all proceed from the same divine com-passion, which always takes the initiative, for we are unable to repent by ourselves. To illustrate, let us look at two of the most powerful episodes of repetition in the Old and New Testaments.

One of the classic moments of prophetic call in the Old Testa-ment is that of Isaiah. Within the context of the divine call, the purification and commissioning of Isaiah take place. On the one hand there is the revelation of divine glory and holiness, and on the other the realization of Isaiah's mortality and sinfulness which brings him to penitence and confession. One can almost hear the incessant chanting of the seraphim calling antiphonally and repetitively to one another:

> *Holy, holy, holy is the Lord of hosts;*
> *The whole earth is full of his glory.* (Isaiah 6:3)

Here is a vision into heaven, a transient glimpse into the unending adoration ascribed to Yahweh in his threefold being and glory. And repetition is woven into the account.

The New Testament apocalypse gives us the second illustration of repetition. Here is another picture of the heavenly court that John beheld 'in the Spirit' (Revelation 4:2). He cannot describe quite what he saw, for the central throne is filled with light and glory and surrounded by an emerald rainbow.

The whole people of God are symbolized by the 24 elders clothed with righteousness and splendour. The four living creatures sur-rounding the throne reflect the divine glory and lead the heavenly worship, which is repetitive in form:

Day and night without ceasing they sing,
'Holy, holy, holy,
the Lord God the Almighty,
who was, and is, and is to come.'
(Revelation 4:8)

The response to such acclamation and adoration, with incense and fire, is the worship offered by the 24 elders who prostrate themselves before the throne, crying:

'You are worthy, our Lord and God,
to receive glory and honour and power,
for you created all things,
and by your will they existed and were created.'
(Revelation 4:11)

The high, dramatic moment is the appearance of the Lamb who has been slain and is now risen and endued with all heavenly power. He becomes the centre of the glory and adoration within this trinitarian revelation, and the song of creation becomes the song of redemption. Myriads upon myriads of adoring creatures, representing all hierarchies and orders of being throughout the whole universe, cry out, time and time again:

'Worthy is the Lamb that was slaughtered
to receive power and wealth and wisdom and might
and honour and glory and blessing!'
Then I heard every creature in heaven and on earth and in the sea,
and all that is in them, singing,
'To the one seated on the throne and to the Lamb
be blessing and honour and glory and might forever and ever!'
And the four living creatures said, 'Amen!'
And the elders fell down and worshipped.
(Revelation 5:12–14)

The point I am making here from Isaiah 6 and from Revelation 4 and 5 is that in this blend of profound penitence and adoring worship there is repetitive expression of both pain and glory. This is initiated by the indwelling Spirit and is both intensely personal and deeply corporate in its expression. The whole order of created and redeemed beings is caught up into such glory, and it flows back to its source in the mystery of God the Father. This is the quality of penitence and adoration that is found in the simplicity and profundity of repetition in the Jesus Prayer.

The lips, the mind, the heart

There are three degrees or stages at which the Prayer may be experienced—the lips, the mind and the heart. They express symbolically and literally the evolution of the Prayer in human experience when directed by the Holy Spirit.

The first stage is to repeat the Prayer audibly with the lips. The mind may be distracted and full of irrelevant desires. Don't be anxious about that, for the Prayer will do its own work under the Holy Spirit. The important thing is that the believer should repeat the name of Jesus with reverence and diligence, whatever the feelings.

In the second stage, the lips are closed. The Prayer moves to the mind, and there is thoughtful attention to the name of Jesus. It is not an exercise in mental concentration; there is no striving to eject other thoughts and no anxious mental effort—just a free, simple awareness of the name of Jesus. Do not strain but gently, simply, always return to the Prayer, return to the Prayer, return to the Prayer.

In the third stage, the Prayer or the name of Jesus moves to the heart. The lips and vocal cords are silent and the mind becomes quiet. The Prayer is lodged in the centre of the being, the cave of the heart. There are many variations of this third stage—from the grace granted to beginners to the mature experience of those who have dwelt within the name of Jesus for many years. The apprenticeship may take the whole of one's life, but within this third stage there are glimpses of complete, quiet resting in God— what the Orthodox call *hesychasm*—the prayer of quiet. All desires are transformed and pass into the sole desire for the Lord—to contemplate his glory and enter more deeply into union with him. Some of the great hesychasts have recommended that it be uttered (though inaudibly) according to the rhythm of respiration or heartbeat. Thus the whole being—body, soul and spirit—is taken up in prayer (1 Thessalonians 5:23), and ultimately the whole universe of which the body is part.

Practice, posture, breathing and heartbeat

We have said that there is a basic simplicity in being still, immersing oneself in the biblical name of Jesus, and repeating the Prayer —and that is all. There are many other ways of praying, of course, and this way is one that does not suit everyone. Indeed, its very simplicity puts some people off. But if you find yourself drawn to its description and have found some meaning in beginning to practise it, then it may well be for you, as Bishop Simon and I affirm its relevance for us. No method or technique can bring about an awareness of God's presence and activity automatically. God is sovereign, free and acts under no compulsion. Prayer is neither magic nor manipulative. Even in the practice of the Jesus Prayer, some find the simple ways best, and others find that the method and technique involving posture, breathing and heartbeat are ways into the precious grace and silence with God. Let me outline the method in a practical way.

First, find a place of quiet where you will not be disturbed (Matthew 6:6). Then, sitting upright using a prayer stool, cushion or with legs crossed, find a posture where you can be relaxed and yet alert. The back should be kept straight.

Use some simple words of faith and affirmation such as 'Breathe on me, breath of God...' and bring yourself into a unity of concentration, relaxing each part of your body from the crown of your head to the soles of your feet. Settle down into this relaxed position and take note of the rate and rhythm of your breathing.

Let your breathing slow down gently and become slightly deeper, breathing from your diaphragm rather than from your chest (belly breathing, not chest breathing).

Note the deep, slow inspiration, the slight pause, the expiration. Follow your breathing, giving attention to regularity with gentleness. Let nothing be forced, but more and more surrender your tensions to the inward work of the Holy Spirit. It is possible, after a few minutes of such relaxed breathing, to begin gently to repeat the Jesus Prayer on the expiration and inspiration of the breath. But let us first take note of the heartbeat.

There is no need to take your pulse, for if you have brought yourself into a posture of relaxation, and your breathing is slow, deep and rhythmic, you may well already be aware of your heartbeat. If you have not done this before, it will take a bit of getting used to, as does every new practice, so it may be a help to take your pulse, counting gently the beats (at rest between 70 and 80 a minute— this varies with individuals). When you are aware of it, then let your mind focus upon the loveliness of Christ as Lord and Saviour, and begin quietly to repeat the words of the Jesus Prayer, according to the heartbeat:

1	Lord	6	have
2	Jesus	7	mercy
3	Christ	8	on
4	Son	9	me
5	of God	10	a sinner (brief pause, then begin again)

You may find this too fast even for a slow, steady pulse, and certainly if you are participating in a group then the leader will regulate the

Prayer at a slower rhythm. It is a matter of practice, and you will find that it is easier to keep the pulse rate with the Prayer when it is said mentally.

Some people find themselves more at home using the Prayer with their outbreaths and inbreaths, remembering that the Holy Spirit is the breath of God. You may proceed:

Inhalation: Lord Jesus Christ
Hold: Son of God
Exhalation: have mercy on me, a sinner

The respiration has already been slowed to a steady and rhythmic rate, and there should be no effort involved in saying the Prayer. It will become clear how important posture, relaxation and sparse, loose clothing are when you are using the heartbeat or breath to accompany the prayer.

The use of a prayer rope with 100 knots, or a string of 50 or 100 wooden beads with one large knot or bead to mark the end, can be useful in a Jesus Prayer group, especially if you are using 100 or 200 repetitions to begin a time of silence. Otherwise, such an aid can be dispensed with, though there are many who use a rope not only for counting but as a means of concentrating and stilling the mind as the fingers move from knot to knot.

This chapter has woven together the fact that the Jesus Prayer is both simple and profound, and has included the practical know-how to begin. It is a self-contained chapter that may be taken as a basic instruction in the practice of the Jesus Prayer. From this point the reader may link up with a soul friend, instructor or group and begin the adventure while allowing the remaining chapters to shed still more light upon the path.

The living fountain that Jesus promised at the feast of Tabernacles springs up in the believer's heart and its fulfilment may well find expression in the practice of the Jesus Prayer: 'Let anyone who is thirsty come to me, and let the one who believes in me drink. As the scripture has said, "Out of the believer's heart shall flow rivers of living water"' (John 7:37–38).

Jesus was speaking of the indwelling Spirit, and it is significant that the word rendered 'heart' in the New Revised Standard Version is translated in different ways in other versions, endeavouring to communicate the idea of the innermost sanctuary of our humanity.

CHAPTER 6

THE JESUS PRAYER AND PERSONAL GROWTH

Bishop Simon writes:

Family likeness

Early on in my working life, and then when I was involved in CMS, and again at Coventry and with the Synod International and Development Affairs Committee, I found myself travelling in various parts of Asia, the Middle East and Africa. During those travels I experienced a phenomenon that I can only call a kind of family likeness! There are always those moments when you meet someone who, by a gesture, a look or a mannerism, suddenly reminds you of someone else quite different in every other respect. In so many ways they may be physically quite unlike, in situation or occupation absolutely different, and yet there is that haunting hint in them of someone else from a totally different setting. You are not surprised when you learn that the person you have just met is a cousin or even a brother or sister of the one that they have been reminding you of so strongly. However elusive the similarity, that strange sense of common identity is present, as if some similar combination of genes was there.

I remember standing in the desert some way outside Omdurman and chatting with a remarkable Sudanese man, perhaps in his fifties, to whom I had been introduced at a late-night picnic under the stars. There was something quite destinctive about his expression. It was the combination of his delighted smile with the quizzical look which the tribal markings incised on his cheeks enhanced by his intense gaze. Somehow that fusion of joy and searchingness instantly recalled someone else, quite other. He was telling me of his pilgrimage through Islam to Christ, of his going out into the desert to wrestle with certain demons he felt within him, and to let them be driven away by the cleansing Spirit of Christ, and then returning to draw a little group around him to study the Bible and the Qur'an.

Afterwards, thinking over that remarkable conversation and the prayer together that followed, I realized whose face I had been recollecting while this new friend was speaking. It was a young Japanese woman, speaking in a school in Japan, and telling us how, after an unhappy upbringing, she had been in such despair that she had flung herself under a train. She had woken to find herself swathed in bandages in a hospital without her legs and without half one arm, but still, to her horror, alive. Members of a small Pentecostal Christian group had come into the ward to visit the patients. Through their loving care she had met with Christ and been given new hope. Later she had married their pastor, and now, with artificial limbs, she was bringing up a family and going out to speak to young people. Her face shone in spite of the gentle gravity of her way of speaking.

But there were others, very many of them, people from every kind of culture and differing continents and ethnic groups, in whom I could discern an instant kinship to the Sudanese man and the Japanese woman. There were obscure people like a young man working with the poorest of the poor in a squatters' settlement in Calcutta, or a South Indian nun teaching in a small school on an island in Bangladesh. There were apostolic leaders like Archbishop Janani Luwum in Uganda, who told me, at the time when he had been leading the bishops in resisting President Amin's brutal cruelty, how he would not last many months more as there were often people lurking in wait to attack him. When I tried to suggest that CMS might get him to leave the country for a while, he refused, declaring that he must stay with his people, and then spoke of how 'the Lord had done a work in his heart' when he was young and had been doing it every day since. That same Lord would be with him whatever befell him. Again I recall how his face shone despite his sombre theme, shone as the face of Stephen, the first martyr, must have shone (Acts 6:15; 7:55).

Then there was Bishop Nathaniel Garang, known as the apostle of the Dinka in the Sudan, at a retreat for the Sudanese bishops in the Church of the Province of Kenya retreat house near Nairobi. He would stride across many miles of devastated terrain to comfort and uphold his shattered people. Emaciated as they were, they rejoiced to see him and danced and sang, waving like spears the long improvised crosses of wood and cartridge cases that were symbols of their new-found faith. On the retreat, he would always be there in the earliest dawn in the place of prayer, as if in a trance, before anyone else was awake, stretched motionless as a pillar of dark wood in his chair. Or again, the bishop's wife from Jinan in China, Jing An, an intrepid woman who had endured solitary confinement in the Cultural Revolution and, with her steadfast husband, Bishop Wang, helped to inspire a new generation in the rapidly growing church. She also had a face that, for all the marks of suffering, had an air of serene composure. In an inner-city or a housing estate congregation in Coventry diocese I could see the same expression of pain mingled with hope, weariness and yet a resilient gleam of welcome on the faces of some of those, black and white, who bear the brunt of the struggle to cope with poverty and deprivation in this country.

What is the key to this 'family likeness'? What is its distinguishing character? I think that it was a long-ago visit to Mother Teresa in her hospice for the dying in Calcutta that gave me the clue. I was awaiting the great lady in a little side-room, when there was the clanking of a bucket outside and someone hurried in—as I thought, to tell me that Mother Teresa was coming. Presently, when the little woman who had entered came up to me, grasped my hand in her damp, roughened one and smiled her welcome, I suddenly realized that this was Mother Teresa herself!

She said how happy she was that I had come and looked as if I, who was unknown and unexpected, were the one person whom she wanted to see. I felt wonderfully received and affirmed. She gave me her whole attention and her eyes looked so completely and so kindly upon me, and yet I suddenly found myself wishing that she wasn't so intently focused on me. I felt that she could see right into me and I was afraid of what she might perceive. And yet at the same moment I knew that she was utterly forgiving and compassionate.

Her expression was one of acceptance. But it was both shrewd and compassionate. You felt that she had seen into the abyss of evil and knew it well, and yet she knew us to be in the firm grasp of a love that had encompassed that evil and absorbed it. In the light of that gaze I would come to see that the family likeness that bound in one all the faces I have described was a coming together of sorrow and gladness, of pain and healing, of judgment and mercy, in such a form that the mercy, the healing and the gladness enveloped their opposites and transfigured them. This is the beauty that we can recognize at once in the saints. It is simply the reflection of a great love, because, truly understood, the saints are simply people, whether ordinary or extraordinary, often weak and certainly fallible, who have really come to know themselves to be held in that love.

As we walked out of the hospice, having seen all the sisters working quietly and happily, it seemed, for those who had been brought in the small man who had taken me in, an eager social worker, turned to me and said, 'Isn't she wonderful? She makes you feel bigger *and* smaller!' That perfectly encapsulated what I was feeling. It was as if I wanted to be different now and even knew that I could be, and this was true of everyone else around me as well! The whole world about us, the bustle of the streets of that teeming city, seemed, for a time at least, enhanced by that conviction.

The tapestry

I thought of all these encounters with many witnesses ('Christ plays in ten thousand places... To the Father through the features of men's faces', in Gerard Manley Hopkins' words—but men's *and* women's faces) when I knelt and looked up at a tremendous representation of Christ on my first entry into Coventry Cathedral on my way to being enthroned there as Bishop. The poet Edwin Muir once wrote in a poem to his beloved, 'Yes, yours my Love was the right human face I, in my mind, had looked for for so long'. I was so nervous that I was only too glad to sink to my knees at the point at which I had been told to. I looked up and saw gazing down upon me from that huge icon, the Sutherland Tapestry, the 'right human face' indeed, the portrayal of 'the glory of God in the face of Jesus Christ' (2 Corinthians 4:6). A special light illuminated the face. The eyes seemed to be looking right into me. Yet even as I might have quailed, the gleam in them could also be felt as almost a twinkle. He seemed to be saying, 'It's all right. I am here with you!'

Long afterwards, I came across some children in the cathedral studying that figure and having an argument about whether he was stern or kind. Eventually, as I stood behind, I heard them agreeing that he was *both*. 'Behold the tenderness and the severity of God' (Romans 11:22)! Here you could say with the psalmist, 'Mercy and truth are met together. Righteousness and peace have kissed each other' (Psalm 85:10, AV).

Surely this is how the disciples saw his glory, 'full of grace *and* truth (John 1:14). Jesus knew what was in them and in all human beings. He knew what they were thinking and what they had been arguing about. They could shrink from his gaze or, like Peter at a supreme moment, once Jesus had looked upon him, 'go out and weep bitterly' (Luke 22:61–62). And yet, they would turn to him in the end: 'Lord, to whom can we go? You have the words of eternal life' (John 6:68).

After I had been to see Pasolini's film of Christ in Matthew's Gospel, a friend coming out of the cinema with me remarked, 'That's just how I pictured Christ: children and swords!' He was one before whom religious leaders and the establishment quailed and yet to whom sinners and children alike went trustingly—and, ultimately, one who on the cross brought together judgment and mercy, the judgment within the mercy, the 'no' within the 'yes'. Here is the ultimate judgment upon our total failure in love. And yet here his arms are stretched out to embrace all, including those who pierced him.

This is what we lack so much in all our relationships. This is what we strive to portray in some of our greatest art and literature, ruthlessly exposing every flaw in human nature and yet with an overarching compassion and pity; and in our greatest music, where the clash between the major and the minor is marvellously sustained and yet ultimately resolved. In the presence of Jesus we find the only place where we can receive and grow into that love which unites justice and mercy. 'Love with its eyes open', Gustav Aulen called it—love that brings home to us both cherishing and, yet, within the cherishing, challenge. Similarly, some German theologians have described God's grace with an untranslatable play on words: *Gabe* (gift) and *Aufgabe* (demand)—but the demand is contained within the gift.

Hesychia

How can we grow into this love until we reflect its fusion of grace and truth? When I lead a Jesus Prayer retreat, the central task is to grow into the practice of the presence of Christ and into communion with him. But this means nothing more or less than to grow in love. 'Love one another as I have loved you' (John 15:12), that is, with the same 'justice-and-mercy' love. But how can we? 'For failing in love is all our travail', as Julian of Norwich said. We try to change but we can't. I recently read a thought by the Revd Jim McEwan, Minister of the parish of Nethybridge in the Church of Scotland, and printed in his parish magazine, adapted from a piece in Anthony de Mello's *The Song of the Bird* (Anand Gujerat Sahitya Prakesh, 1982, p. 67):

For years people told me I should change. I resented them even though I agreed with them! Who were they to tell me what I should be like?

I read in the Bible about how we should be, and imagined God joining in and telling me to change.

Then one day I read again about Jesus' death for sinners, which meant me. I was struck by Paul's words that 'it was while we were still sinners that Christ died for us'. He didn't wait until we had changed.

And suddenly the penny dropped. It dawned on me that I did not need to change for God to love me. And I relaxed. I stopped trying to change. And of course in stopping I found I had begun to change!

So we need above all to let ourselves be held in Jesus' love and let his presence in the Holy Spirit keep breaking and remoulding us. A friend described how she tried to defrost her fridge, chipping away at the ice and pouring boiling water over it to melt and remove it. But it would not budge. It reminded her of some resentments in her heart at that time. She came back to it two hours later and the ice was all melted and gone. So the warmth of God's love 'in Christ' could melt the resentments away, though she could not get rid of them. Jesus told us to 'dwell' or 'abide' in his love. He said that 'without me you can do nothing' (John 15:4–5).

And this is where the continuing practice of saying the Jesus Prayer for a definite time each morning (and evening, when possible) comes in. You can read the day's Bible reading (perhaps BRF's *New Daylight* or *Guidelines*) and say your usual prayers (as an Anglican I like to use the new or the old Prayer Book version). Then, on your own, read a little of some inspiring book, perhaps even one about the Jesus Prayer itself. And then, asking the Holy Spirit to help you and turning to the hard slog (prayer is often a slog) of 'the practice of the presence of Christ', look to him and say the Prayer 'with your mind in your heart', that is, thinking of Christ and receiving from him and longing for more.

The Jesus Prayer can make the 'dwelling' in him more of a firm reality and less of a vague intention. As we keep on turning our thought and feeling back to him, we trust ourselves to his love for us, even when we can't feel it, and look to him to enfold us and those we bring to him more fully in his love. We keep trying gently to drop all the other contents of our mind—what early writers on the Jesus Prayer used to call *logismoi* (thoughts), worries, cares and desires, and to pull away from them. Gradually the Prayer embeds itself in our consciousness throughout the day and often at night. It is good to go to sleep with it and to wake with it. Sometimes, as the Russian pilgrim found, the prayer wakes you: 'Early one morning the Prayer woke me, as it were' (*The Way of A Pilgrim*, SPCK, 1930, p. 26.) Church Fathers and Mothers also spoke of exercising vigilance or watchfulness (*nepsis*) during the day to guard the mind and heart from harmful thoughts, temptations and thoughts that fall short of love, such as resentment, unkindness and, of course, lust, which turns others into objects and ceases to pray for them as people (one may give thanks for beauty or attractiveness without trying to possess it).

The real remedy for such distortions is, as all the most perceptive of the old and more recent writers make clear, is to 'bind the mind with one thought only', or 'the thought of One only' (Bishop Theophan in *The Art of Prayer: An Orthodox Anthology*, Faber, 1966, p. 97). This means that as we keep being drawn back to the presence and person of Christ, the expulsive power of a superior affection will very gradually free us more from the constant stream of thoughts and images that will always tend to beset us. Sometimes at least we shall experience the way in which Jesus himself, by his presence, will, as we call on his name, help to draw the fragments of our divided selves back together round him.

So we will gradually grow into dwelling more and more in him. This indwelling is the heart of *hesychia*, literally 'stillness' or 'being still'. Gradually, in the time of the Desert Fathers and Mothers, it came to mean being united with God through prayer, or indeed being held in his love. It would gradually involve a change of lifestyle, the deliberate giving up of certain habits or attitudes that are shown up in the light of God's love as inadequate, a real reorientation. I am not thinking of a puritanical obsession with every detail but of shaping one's whole life into a greater integrity and consistency. We have to learn to think and act as those who live in the light of Christ's constant presence.

This leads us into a continuous turning to Christ in our life as in our prayer, the constant exercise of what the Desert Fathers and Mothers called *penthos*—sorrow over our own personal sins against love and also the wider sins of our society. Watchfulness becomes the kind of vigilance that would have prevented Christians long ago, and certainly in Germany in the 1930s, from generating and also colluding with anti-semitism and racism. We will experience repentance for the many evils of Christendom—for our arrogance and insensitivity to those of other faiths and cultures; for our participation in the Crusades; for our part in fomenting conflicts, sometimes between Christians; for our acceptance of a way of life that promotes greed and competitiveness and connives at the injustice and the poverty in our society and across the world; and above all for our role in fostering the prejudice and scapegoating that led to the Holocaust. This is true 'joyful mourning' (John Climacus)—both the source and the fruit of letting the Jesus Prayer stream through us all the time.

Hesychia, then, is primarily living in a constant relationship of penitence and trust in God's love in Christ. It is not only to pray but to let our whole lives become a prayer, prayed in the Spirit. As John Climacus wrote before the Jesus Prayer emerged in its present form, 'Stillness is worshipping God unceasingly and waiting on Him. Let the remembrance of Jesus be present with your every breath. Then indeed you will appreciate the value of stillness (*hesychia*)' (*The Ladder of Divine Ascent*, SPCK, 1982, p. 270). Here already is the seed of the way of prayer that was eventually to prove such an effective way of being drawn into a growing relationship with God in Christ, held in his 'judgment-and-mercy' love and so enabled to be changed into his likeness more and more.

For this to happen, we do not need to go into the desert. Our 'cell' can be a small prayer corner or anywhere that we go to pray. Indeed some of the greatest writers on this theme agree that we can, by making time and quiet to pray, make our body itself into a cell. 'With the mind in the heart', that is with a united being, we can move into the Prayer and enter into the depths of God's love for us and so begin to be changed and to pray for that change to become universal. Judgment-and-mercy love means the love Jesus brought to us, by which we can rejoice in his acceptance now and yet keep looking to be transformed. As the Prayer enables us to grow into this indwelling, we can hear Jesus saying to each one of us, as he said to his disciple, Simon, 'You *are* Simon. You *will be* Peter.' Everywhere God will multiply those who are always growing into his love and reflecting that love in their faces and in their lives and their shared life.

CHAPTER 7

THE JESUS PRAYER AND SOLITUDE

Brother Ramon writes:

Some years ago, I had a warm letter from Esther Rantzen inviting me to participate in a TV programme on loneliness and solitude. Most of the programme was to be devoted to the many people who live a kind of emotional isolation caused by their own interior problems and the society that rejects them at so many levels. Included also would be those who, through force of circumstances, sickness or old age, live in 'high-rise loneliness', isolated in the middle of the community, perhaps in a literal 'high-rise' tower block.

Such people, who represented the isolation and loneliness part of the programme's agenda, would have taken up most of the time. But Esther Rantzen also wanted someone who actually chose solitude as a positive lifestyle, enhancing both their personal and communal way of being and living. She turned to me, realizing that for the reason of my hermit vocation I might not want to take part in such a programme. I did not participate, but we had an excellent and perceptive exchange of letters.

It is true to say that we are born alone and that we die alone. And if we are to be truly human we should not only grow into loving human relationships but also learn the true solitude that comes from facing ourselves. In this way we may become rich in God, and our human friendships and relationships will function warmly and positively in the world. If we embrace our creaturely solitude in this way, we shall not end up as frightened or bored ciphers, merely existing in an indifferent world. There are many ways in which this can be done, and the way of the Jesus Prayer has proved to me a primary way of being and praying that helps to accomplish this very thing. Let me give you a glimpse into my experience of geographical solitude, which may not be possible for you but may shed some light upon your path.

After I had spent six positive months of spring and summer solitude in Dorset in the early 1980s, I sensed a pressing call to repeat it a year or so later. Mother Mary Clare SLG was then my spiritual director and she gently but insistently guided me towards this more demanding confrontation with my own solitude, the next step to what eventually became a hermit vocation. As a contrast to the first gentle period of solitude, I now needed wild mountain terrain, bleak cold days and nights with the winds, storms and heaving sea reflecting winter's heaviness, darkness and mystery. This landed me on the tip of the Lleyn peninsula on the North Wales coast, facing the powerful island of Bardsey, the 'island of 20,000 saints'—tiny as it is—where, in medieval times, three pilgrimages there were worth one to Jerusalem. I wrote to Mother Mary Clare in my first report from there:

Darkness and mist fall over the mountain, the cry of the high wind echoes around the cottage and the dim outlines of the surrounding rocky heights bear witness to the austerity of the months to come. But the mystic fire burns within, and the longing for the Beloved and the pain of absence mingle in the way that opens before me.

As to Bardsey itself, it served to underline my solitude and solidarity with all people on earth and within the communion of saints. Sometimes the facing island loomed dark and menacing out of the turbulent waters. Sometimes it would catch and reflect the glorious sunset over still and golden sea. But always, as the island of 20,000 saints, it possessed a quality of the numinous, of awe and mystery —and a spiritual quality that was threatening as well as glorious. I felt the peninsula in its pagan as well as its Christian setting. The whole feel of the place not only changed with my changing moods, but I felt that it sometimes imposed its own mood upon me. Contemporary writers on Christian spirituality speak of Bardsey island and the Lleyn peninsula with great awe and reverence. It is certainly one of the remaining secluded holy places of the Christian tradition. It was in this place of enforced solitude that the Jesus Prayer ministered to me in preparation for further evolution of my vocation.

Integration of solitude and solidarity

I found myself on my prayer stool in the 4.30am darkness of each morning, fingering the first 100 knots of my prayer rope, remembering the words I had heard at the St David's Hermit Symposium that had so marked my life back in 1975:

There are always likely to be some men and women who feel that 'material' solitude is essential for their spiritual life. They can no more do without it than without food or drink, and if they are deprived of this isolation their lives become spoilt, cramped and distorted and they never find their true vocations. The 'born solitary' is drawn to an eremitical life for various reasons, partly natural, partly supernatural… They discover that they need to separate themselves from their fellow creatures in order that their latent powers may have room for expansion and growth, that they be more fitted to serve mankind generally.

The above words come from Peter Anson, and Mother Mary Clare gave her own perspective at the same symposium:

The hermit is simply a pioneer… in the way of the desert which the whole of humanity must follow of necessity one day, each one according to measure and desire. This eremitical vocation, at least embryonically, is to be found in every Christian vocation, but in some it must be allowed to come to its full flowering in the wind of the Spirit. It is not enough to affirm that the thing is good in itself, it is necessary that the Church and society do something, so that this life be realizable, so that each may at least touch it, be it only with the tip of his little finger.

It is difficult quite to say *how* the continued, daily and persistent practice of saying the Prayer actually carries you down into such awareness and confrontation with God that begins to answer the basic question 'Who am I?' But it does so, and it doesn't stop there. It traverses the deep places of the human spirit, and enables the pilgrim to continue the quest into the broader, deeper, higher places of our humanity. We thus explore such solidarity and prove that in fact 'no one is an island'. We all belong to one another.

The first chapters of Genesis may not be literally factual, but they are theologically and spiritually true and inspired. They teach us the basic unity of the human race, so that when we truly understand, theologically and spiritually, that we are one in Adam, then we understand the Adam–Christ parallel that is so important in the teaching of the apostle Paul (Romans 5:12–21; 1 Corinthians 15:21–22, 45). We are truly one in Christ, and he becomes our representative not only in our humanity but in the cosmic work of redemption. This teaching floods the human race with hope in Jesus, in ultimate union with the trinitarian life of God.

Your cell will teach you all things

It is the glory of being human that we can do this very thing— explore the solitary wonders and wastes of our humanity. There is immense risk as well as glory in all this, of course, as open to our destruction as to our salvation, if it were not for the saving grace of the Holy Spirit.

I have said that I have been practising and teaching the Jesus

Prayer for well over twenty years, and this has carried me deeper both into the solitary and corporate nature of our lives. During the same period I have been inspired by the life and pilgrimage of Thomas Merton, whose life seemed prematurely cut off in December 1968 during a monastic conference in Bangkok. I explored his life and teaching for most of my post-graduate work.

A great deal of Merton's contemplative teaching had to do with our concerns in this book, but the revival and popularity of the Jesus Prayer had not developed much in the West before his death, for I would have been so excited about the way he would have taken it up and taught it in his own tradition, as I feel sure he would have done. Up on the Lleyn peninsula I took his book *Contemplation in a World of Action* (Unwin, 1980), in which is included his powerful essay 'The Cell'. It is based upon the story of a novice among the Desert Fathers who could not deal with his loneliness. He had been doing his best to cope with what he felt were the demands of the ascetic and spiritual life, and realized that he was no monk but a simple human being who could not pray or love or deal with a confrontation with himself, let alone with God.

When he brought all this to the wise old Abba (father), the counsel he received was that he was simply to sit in his cell dwelling on the name of God, and his cell would teach him all things.

In telling the story in his essay, Merton adds:

Patiently putting up with the incomprehensible unfulfilment of the lonely, confined, silent, obscure life of the cell, we gradually find our place, the spot where we belong as monks: that is, of course, solitude, the cell itself. This implies a kind of mysterious awakening to the fact that where we actually are is where we actually belong, namely in solitude, in the cell. Suddenly we see 'this is it'.

And of course this is not just for monks or Desert Fathers, but for ordinary human beings. And the wonderful thing is that it is not narcissistic but wholesomely communal if you let the Jesus Prayer do its work, and this means letting the indwelling Holy Spirit manifest God's love in you. Wherever I have observed a dedicated team of people work together towards a greater goal, I see this principle in operation, for it is a natural one as well as a spiritual one, whether the team is dedicated to the arts, science, or a research project in medicine, music, theology or spirituality. When it works in the religious life it is something very beautiful.

For instance, I have had good reason to observe closely the teamwork that has drawn me into its healing process over the last eighteen months in my serious illness. The 'pain resolution' team has a Macmillan nurse leader who is a perceptive and dedicated woman, who knows her job as well as her team! The way they have set before them 'the one thing needful' has clearly shown the dedication and integration of the personal and the corporate. And the result has not only been the accomplishment of the task in my own profound need, but the confidence and sense of well-being that they have stimulated in me in the observation of this principle. The same has been the case moving from the consultant through the GP and nursing team from the medical centre.

I have talked over this point with some of the team, and they have been intrigued by my observations within their own practice and in the life here in the monastery at Glasshampton, and also about the way in which I am now able to write about this whole principle of integrated teamwork. It is well based because it is psychologically sound, for a holistic approach is applicable at all levels of human team functioning, and applies as much to the Jesus Prayer as to the functioning of a well-regulated team.

Of course, lots of such teams do not work because of human sin, frailty or bad organization, with bureaucratic demands and workloads. That is when there is need for the application of solid, logical thinking and a built in 'conflict resolution' pattern. At that point in our mutual sharing, we chuckle and confess that all is not as rosy as it appears from outside, and that we need a dose of human humility and the grace of God's forgiveness.

Before we leave Merton's essay, I want to mention that when I placed it in parallel with St Francis' counsel on the same pattern, they both fused with the practice of the Jesus Prayer in a marvellous manner. In Merton's words:

Our body is our cell. Wherever we are, wherever we go, we bring our cell with us. Our brother body is our cell and our soul is the hermit living in that cell in order to pray to God and meditate. If our soul does not live in peace and solitude within its cell, of what avail is it to live in a man-made cell?

Merton says that it is the person and presence of Jesus that integrates the personal and corporate, the solitude and the communal in the life of prayer and love:

He reveals his Name as that of JESUS, Saviour, in whom and with whom I am one with all people. Thus my place as intercessor and brother is also my solitude and my cell where I find and love all people in the warm and human love of the presence of Christ, for it is the Word Incarnate... who alone can give me full comfort in trials that are essentially human and bound up with my physical being.

I write from my vantage point of over ten years as a hermit brother, as Bishop Simon writes from a varied ministry in the priestly, missionary and episcopal care of God's people—but it is as two human beings that we collaborate in our writing because we have been fired and enthused by our practice of the Jesus Prayer. And we want to share it in all its depths and heights, with you whose life may be falling into disintegration, or who conversely may feel that God is drawing you to a deeper, fuller and more wonderful quest into the mystery of his own trinitarian love.

CHAPTER 8

THE JESUS PRAYER
AND THE LOCAL CHURCH

Bishop Simon writes:

The true vine

In writing about the family likeness that marked a whole variety of saints throughout the world, I mentioned a Chinese woman, Jing An, the wife of Bishop Stephen Wang of Jinan. She and he, together with one of the senior pastors from his diocese, were among a whole circle of remarkable people from different countries and continents who came to the diocese of Coventry not long after I had arrived. They came as part of a 'Call to Mission in Partnership' that summoned the parishes and people of the diocese to join with the world Church in mission. This little group, meeting at our diocesan retreat house at Offchurch, seemed to bear that same 'family likeness' themselves. Coming from Wales, from India, from South Africa and Holland and the United States, and from what was then East Germany, from South Africa, and from Barbados, they were a remarkable group of women and men all of whom inspired and challenged us. But it was the Chinese contingent who, encouraged by the others on the team, put the striking comment to us that gave the message of the group its central theme. They said, 'You have good resources, many talents and interesting initiatives, but you are all rooted in many different vines.

You must learn, as we have had to, to abide in the true vine, to deepen your trust in him and enlarge your love for each other and for those around you.'

A year or two later, the bishop's immediate team, the suffragan (assistant) bishop and the two archdeacons, were meeting at the retreat house in the same room where the visitors had sat, wrestling with something of their legacy. We had been asked by the Bishop's Council, the standing committee of the diocesan synod, to go aside and work together at a mission statement for the diocese. There had already been two general appeals for reports and views on our mission from the parishes, in my own time and my predecessor's, and people felt that they didn't want any more such processes. They asked the leaders to review all the previous contributions and then to come out with a vision of the goal for the diocese and the parishes as a whole.

After we had discussed and prayed into the night, we went to bed with a tangle of diagrams and phrases on our whiteboard. Early next morning, however, one of the group came down and drew it all into one shape. We had decided that there would be no statement, no pages of diocesan-speak, just one symbol and a few words, a pattern rather than a paper. This was just what a similar team had produced at CMS some years earlier. Then it was called (appropriately, since the first great General Secretary of CMS was Henry Venn!) a 'Venn' diagram of concentric circles. Now it was the Mercian Cross, a symbol still used by the dioceses in the area that was once Anglo-Saxon Mercia, first evangelized by St Chad from Lindisfarne.

Originally it must have had a circle round it, and really should have had again, symbolizing movement and flexibility and the interplay of all its parts. Now it was still a cross with a square in the centre and squares at its head and its foot and at the end of each arm. A common urge of the Spirit gave us all together, instantly, the theme for the centre. There was no question about it. The words of the Chinese, the conviction that united us all, the spiritual hunger of our society and of our whole church, made it so plain. We must begin with a movement of prayer to the Father through the Son, in the Spirit, a prayer of abiding in the true vine—or, in Ephesian and Colossian terms, being rooted and grounded in love, rooted in Christ. So we set 'rooted in Christ' (Ephesians 3:17, AV, combined with Colossians 2:7) at the centre. The Jesus Prayer would have been the perfect expression of this kind of prayer. Although I hesitated in any way to impose it, yet I longed for it. 'Lord Jesus Christ, Son of God, have mercy upon us!'

We also placed on the central square the Cross of Nails, symbol of Christ's reconciliation and healing. This had emerged as a symbol for the diocese on the morning after the bombing of the cathedral in 1940. It became the embodiment of the vision given to Provost Howard in the previous night as he stood watching his cathedral burn. He had seen Christ suffering with us and summoning us all through this brokenness to reach out towards a new wholeness lying far beyond the war, a *shalom* peace towards which we must always labour. In this struggle we were to be strengthened by the One who had gone through disintegration for us and opened up for us the possibility of being made whole. 'Lord Jesus Christ, Son of God, have mercy upon us!'

Life together and ministry together

Now, as the bishop's team reflected in our retreat house, we looked to that redemptive tree, planted in the midst of our shattered world. We opened ourselves to the presence. And the arms of the Mercian cross opened out into the two ways in which prayer and abiding in the vine would flower and bear fruit in the parishes and the diocese and more widely.

First, on the square on the left-hand end of the cross, we put the phrase 'Life together'. This was to symbolize the healing of relationships through mutual forgiveness and repentance. It would mean that as people prayed more deeply, there would spring up an urge to overcome all criticisms, resentments, hostilities and cliquishness, to transcend the contrast between ethnic groups and social classes, wealthy and poor, old inhabitants and newcomers, conservative and radical, and those of different parishes, denominations, churchmanships.

These barriers could only be melted down and changed in the white radiant heat of the divine love as people really and truly gave themselves to prayer. And the wealthier and poorer parts of towns and, indeed, of villages and rural areas, of the city of Coventry, and the north and the south of the diocese and the county—divided as far back as the Wars of the Roses, then in the Civil War, and the Industrial Revolution and its aftermath—would care about each other and bear each other's burdens. The tears of a headteacher struggling in a primary school on a vast, neglected housing estate in Nuneaton, or of an unemployed woman who had once again been deprived of her job, would burn on the cheeks of those in large houses like my own 'Bishop's House', in comfortable suburbs, or in one of the more prosperous villages. The boredom of young people with little to do except gather together sometimes even round the church gates and express their frustration, the helplessness of young single parents and children who had known no love or care, and had few role models or little hope for the future, would weigh upon the more prosperous and powerful. And there would be a new atmosphere of caring for each other and ministering to each other among all.

Lord Jesus Christ, Son of God, have mercy upon us!

On the square at the end of the right-hand end of the cross we wrote 'Ministry together', symbolizing a movement of the Spirit that would give power and fruitfulness to this movement of *agape* love, by affirming and releasing the gifts of laity and clergy alike, by inspiring more and more people with the confidence to develop the skills to care for each other and contribute to the community, to help with the young, to support other people at work or work with others to create new jobs. We saw this as a movement of creative co-operation between clergy and laity, parishes and congregations of all churches and denominations, reaching out into the whole community and bringing with it a new sense of potential and hope.

Lord Jesus Christ, Son of God, have mercy upon us!

Witness to the world and witness in the world

In the square at the top of the Mercian Cross we wrote the words 'Witness to the World'. This again arose naturally from the way in which the central square—the contemplation of Christ and being rooted in him in prayer and worship—held together the other two squares at either end of the cross-bar, repentance and forgiveness on the left and the release of the gifts of the Spirit on the right. A church sharing this humbling on the one side and affirming on the other would combine a quality of constant openness to forgiveness, a readiness to be humbled on the one hand and on the other the capacity to be lifted up in the renewing power of God's love. Such a church would have a quality of life, a quality of relationships, that could constitute a lens through which those coming into that church's corporate life would be able to discern Christ and be drawn to him. They would see in this church what it means to die with Christ and to be raised up in him.

We need our churches to become the kind of places to which we could gladly take a friend who is a complete outsider to the church, because the kind of welcome they would receive and the kind of worship they would experience would have a depth and genuineness and openness that could truly constitute a kind of homecoming. Here would be some kind of anticipation of the goal towards which humanity itself is struggling. A church rooted and grounded in prayer and in the hidden contemplation of the presence of Christ would have a powerful attraction to it. The sense of the love of God poured out would be palpable, not because the members were trying self-consciously to make it so, but because they were naturally, gently and easily held in that love by the stream of prayer that flowed through their shared life.

The most important features of such a shared life would be inwardly a complete honesty and humility, with a readiness to forgive and to receive forgiveness, and outwardly a strong compassion and concern for all fellow beings, especially those who were suffering, struggling or in need. It would combine the fruit of the Spirit, a mutual love, with the release of gifts to minister to the needs of others.

The best kinds of Christian community, *and* some of the most apparently ordinary, vulnerable and struggling little churches all over the world, not least in our own cities and villages, can develop something of the character of the 'base community', as the churches of the poor in South America and parts of Africa and Asia have been called. They can have an immediate, quite unconscious converting power about them. Some of the best Alpha or Emmaus groups have had the same corporate appeal. As they say when you arrive in the Orthodox monastery that Brother Ramon and I have so much enjoyed visiting, 'Christ is amongst us!' And the response is, 'He is and ever shall be.'

Finally, in the square at the base of the cross we inscribed the parallel phrase, 'Witness *in* the world'. This was to describe the way in which the members of such churches would be enabled by the Spirit to respond to the world in which they live and work, to learn from its struggles and, as they enter into the worlds of people very different from themselves, to discern the form Christ is taking in those worlds.

This will happen as we let the Jesus Prayer keep flowing through our life and consciousness, opening us up to the questions and hopes and longings of those around us. What we need ourselves, above all, is a strong centre but a wide circumference. All over the world the Church seems static and contained, or even tired and declining, where it is set in its habitual, conventional Westernized culture. On the other hand, the Church seems vital and growing where:

- it is true to its own spiritual source and yet alert to the culture, dreams and potential of those outside it;

- it is active within the reshaping of our contemporary society in all its diversity, as it reaches out towards some kind of 'unity in diversity', a shared corporate goal for humanity.

These requirements will involve being ready to move out into the melting-pot of religions, of new patterns in the arts, the writing and music and the information technology of the 21st century. We need the gifts and aptitudes to capture the imagination of a new generation. We need the prophetic and critical capacity to help our contemporaries break beyond the tyranny of our market-driven society. So much of so called postmodernism is only a phase in late capitalism, a philosophy of the market shaped and constrained by the market. We need the breadth of sympathy to discern Christ in unexpected places and to link up with a strange variety of allies, whether in the business world, among scientists, among artists or indeed among followers of the 'New Age'.

In all this exploration, we must be kept constantly in the presence of Christ, open to his judgment and mercy, seeing in him our true goal, and acknowledging that only in being held in his love and constantly returning to him can we be open to the ideals of some of our contemporaries but aware of possible illusions. We must remain vigilant but patient, opposed to any tendency to 'drop out' from society into some kind of sectarian or spiritual half-world. We must recognize the proneness to sin and self-seeking among the most utopian, and the potential for good among even the most worldly. Then we will recognize that social institutions, political, civil and religious institutions, with all their ambiguity, are vitally necessary. Our task is to stay with them, not to opt out. They can veil privilege and abuse of power but they can also preserve values and protect from chaos. Held in Christ's love, we must stay within these institutions and labour to change them continually. We must through his Spirit generate a culture and a politics of forgiveness, perpetual repentance and continuing hope—'joyful mourning' indeed!

We certainly want to awaken within the Church itself a quickened awareness of Christ's presence. We need to develop today a very different form of Christianity from that which has prevailed in the West hitherto. We need the kind of Christianity that has more of the character of monastic renewal at its simplest and freshest, in both West and East. We need the character of Celtic mission, of the early Franciscans, of some aspects of the radical reformation of the 16th century, of basic Christian communities among the poor all over the world, of the marriage of East and West in Christian ashrams in Asia, more open to deep exchange between people of differing faiths in search of peace and justice. Such a Church would be far less hier-archical or bureaucratic, deeply repentant of racism, exclusivism, complacent triumphalism and rigidity, open to the feminine and to full scope for women, revering the natural world and richly trini-tarian. Held in the love of Christ and open to the stream of the Spirit and the prayer that prays itself within and among us, we can be changed and keep being changed more into his likeness.

Follow-up

This was something of the vision symbol that we took out into the diocese, which is still being realized and still will be for a long time to come, no doubt in new forms and under different names. When I left, we had barely scratched the surface and it is still no doubt a long way from penetrating into the whole life of diocese or parishes. But I know that much more has been accomplished in recent times than we had dreamt of then.

One failure in our presentation from the start in those days, in spite of the wide welcome and enthusiastic support that so many people and parishes gave, was that we did not sufficiently empha-size the crucial place of prayer. A 'spirituality group' and their team have done a great deal and the retreat house is a wonderfully positive resource through which we were all influenced. But in the life of our whole Church, and in the lives of all of us, including myself, prayer has still not taken the absolutely central position that it must if the whole movement of new life and mission is to take off. The simple words have still not resonated sufficiently deeply in our minds and hearts, 'Without me you can do nothing.' We have still to focus on that 'abiding'.

I believe that a widespread development of the practice of the Jesus Prayer and a fuller recognition of how it can bring a renewed relationship with God in Christ through the Spirit could really bring about significant change. Dietrich Bonhoeffer, faced with the tragic failure of the German Church to stand up against Nazism was driven to call and work for a new beginning. He even took a group of young future pastors aside to his own 'alternative' seminary at Finkenwalde, and nurtured them in a community of rootedness in Christ and mutual confession and forgiveness. Later, in prison, he called for the Church to become capable of a palpable and visible life in Christ through a deep hidden growth into prayer and radical action. He wanted us to learn how to be caught up into a new kind of Christian living in the world. Only thus, he believed, could the German Church regain credibility.

In Coventry, we started in a small way when groups from each deanery in the diocese came to the Bishop's House for an evening and gathered for prayer in our beautiful chapel, which was large enough to hold them all. First we had a half hour of silent prayer together, after I had explained briefly how that silence might be used. Only gradually and tentatively, I have to confess, did I introduce the Jesus Prayer, said aloud only by myself, as in the monastery, but entered into by all and culminating in silence. Over the next half hour, people brought up small candles and spoke single-sentence prayers of intercession, placing their candles on a tray on a large altar. We ended with a collect, a prayer that literally 'collects up' the aspirations of all for a particular time in a short classical form. It was as simple as that. And yet, as people left, they often said how much it had meant. I always replied with delight, 'You could do this in your church!'

A number of people started such gatherings, both clergy and laity. I was struck by the effect of such gatherings in little groups in country parishes, as well as on housing estates of increasing numbers of people entering into contemplative prayer. A corporately led saying of the Jesus Prayer, with perhaps some teaching of its rich tradition and meaning, culminating in a time of silence, could lead such groups into spreading a deeper relationship with the living Christ into the whole parish and area. As more and more people become drawn into that stillness, that *hesychia*, across the country, I have no doubt that the power of the Prayer would become a converting force, bringing unknown fullness of life. There would need to be a good deal of teaching and guidance, of course. That is essential if what is happening is to be properly understood. But that can easily be provided. Once more and more people in or around the churches become drawn into this kind of 'dwelling' in God's love, they will find that 'love unknown'. Once we are really exposed to it, it can and does change us.

CHAPTER 9

THE JESUS PRAYER AND INTERCESSION

Brother Ramon writes:

Moved by the Spirit

I am writing these words this morning because of a distinct action of what I believe was the Holy Spirit during the night hours. At 1am I was awakened to think and pray. This is not unusual, and I have come to accept it as part of the way in which I find response in my heart, sometimes to my own longing for God and sometimes to those for whom I pray. But last night it lasted for two hours and then more, and was centred around those amazing verses of Romans 8:26–27 where the Holy Spirit is mentioned four times:

The Spirit helps us in our weakness; for we do not know how to pray as we ought, but that very Spirit intercedes with sighs too deep for words. And God, who searches the heart, knows what is the mind of the Spirit, because the Spirit intercedes for the saints according to the will of God.

I had no option then but to get up and record a synopsis of what was being sounded plainly in my heart and mind, ready to write up this morning. And this is what I now do, and it constitutes this chapter of the book. For if there is any scripture passage that carries me deeper into the practice of the Jesus Prayer it is those words quoted above from the whole context of Romans 8:18–27. I shall try to describe the night experience.

When I awoke in the middle of the night, I found that my customary sense of passive waiting upon God was already in place and all I had to do was to surrender heart and mind into what was being said before entering into an intercessory use of the Jesus Prayer.

First there was the acknowledgment of human weakness, not simply that I was too ignorant to enter into the deep intercession of getting into and under the world's personal and corporate pain, but the realization that I would collapse under such a load because of my human frailty—apart from the regulative measure that the Spirit would impart.

Second, because of that very situation, the Spirit took the initiative and imparted not only the way into intercession by 'sighs too deep for words' and the use of the Jesus Prayer, but by using my whole being as an intercessory channel. I explain this and the following point below.

Third, there was the amazing insight that what was happening was that the divine Spirit was communing with my human spirit—God with God within the human heart.

And fourth, in fulfilment of Romans 8:26–27, the Spirit was actually interceding for the saints (God's redeemed people) according to the will of God.

As I was being carried through such an understanding step by step, it was actually happening within me as I lay there. It was not that I had to make any decisions, take any steps or set in motion any kind of technique or method or contemplative practice. No! All I had to do was to surrender, remain passive, listen, and allow the Spirit to perfect the work within me. And how was that being accomplished? By allowing the Lord to carry me through those two hours and then learning still more by taking me into the Jesus Prayer in its intercessory form:

Lord Jesus Christ
Son of God
have mercy on us.

Of course, this 'us' included myself as one of those within its embrace, so before I could do that I had to remember the following:

- The Jesus Prayer is rooted in the personal, so that although the form was 'us', I was personally and wholly committed to it in the ground of my being.
- Moving out from the personal as individual, I entered into a corporate sense of intercession (friends, loved ones, afflicted human beings in sickness, torture and persecution).
- The Prayer was directed *towards* holy and good corporate power structures demonstrating compassion, and *against* evil structures bound together for profit, violence and evil.

I was then carried back to the Romans text as a manifestation of the Spirit's cosmic work of intercession in the world. This not only led on to a consideration of what the Spirit is accomplishing now, but pointed towards the *parousia*, or coming glory of Christ's ultimate victory.

This took the whole two hours (though I was not counting time!), and at that point I took up my prayer rope and began with the simple personal form of the Jesus Prayer, moving into the intercessory form, and this led to the 'sighs too deep for words'. The prayer ceased to be said verbally and became a matter of the mind and the heart.

It was then after 3am and I was lying on my bed in darkness and silence while the presence of God's intercessory love and power was felt within and without. I don't know how long this went on, but I remember being responsive to the apostle's words in Colossians 1:24: 'I am now rejoicing in my sufferings for your sake, and in my flesh I am completing what is lacking in Christ's afflictions for the sake of his body, that is, the church.' These words do not mean, of course, that anything is lacking in the finished work of Christ in his death and resurrection, but that the risen Lord is so indwelling the redeemed Paul that he is being 'prayed through'. He is being used as a channel, an instrument of the Spirit's interceding power. God within is praying to God above.

In my own experience of the hours of this night, the Spirit caught me up into that kind of intercession. It was a sheer gift, to lead me further and deeper and to enable me to share with you the path that God opens up before us in the practice of the Jesus Prayer.

Intercession includes the world

As Bishop Simon and I maintain, personal and group intercession is part of the whole life of prayer for the baptized Christian within the sacramental and liturgical pattern of the Church's worship. Therefore the practice of the Jesus Prayer enhances the praying life of the Christian, and it leads not only to personal intercession for the afflicted and needy of the world, but is pointed towards the cosmic transfiguration of the world when our Lord returns in glory.

That night-time experience described above is just another stepping-stone for me in this pilgrimage that I have been making for many years, and it only manifests the continuity that has followed me from my early busy evangelical and teaching ministry. Before I began the more serious following of the hermit life in 1990, I had longed for this deeper life, and words from my small booklet *Praying the Jesus Prayer* (Marshall Pickering, 1988) round off this chapter and maintain the continuity. So I reproduce them here.

THE COSMIC NATURE OF THE JESUS PRAYER

We have seen that the Jesus Prayer involves body, mind and spirit. If the whole person is given to God then it reflects the greatest command-ment of all, the command to love: 'Hear, O Israel: The Lord our God the Lord is one; and you shall love the Lord your God with all your heart, and with all your soul, and with all your mind, and with all your strength.' The cosmic nature of the Prayer means that the believer lives as a human being in solidarity with all other human beings, and with the animal creation, together with the whole created order (the cosmos). All this is drawn into and affected by the Prayer. One believer's prayers send out vibrations and reverberations that increase the power of the divine Love in the cosmos.

The Christian is well aware of the fact that the world is also evil. There is a falseness and alienation which has distracted and infected the world, and men and women of prayer, by the power of the Name of Jesus, stand against the cosmic darkness, and enter into conflict with dark powers. *'For we are not contending against flesh and blood, but against the principalities, against the powers, against the rulers of this present darkness, against the spiritual hosts of wickedness in the heavenly places.'* The power of the Jesus Prayer is the armour against the wiles of the devil, taking heed of the apostle's word, *'Pray at all times in the Spirit, with all prayers and supplication.'*

If you persevere with the Prayer it will root itself within your heart by the power of the Holy Spirit and a gentle flame will begin to burn, a bubbling spring will arise, and you will actually find that the apostolic injunction *'Pray without ceasing'* will become part of your life. When you wake in the morning the Prayer will echo in your being; as you go about your daily work the quiet flame will be burning; as you relate to people and situations the spring will be bubbling; as you enter into the resolution of conflicts, meet problems, encounter difficulties, the holy Name will be sounding. As you live in love and truth and spread hope around, the power of the Prayer will energize you, and as you go to bed at night the mighty Name of Jesus will guard and keep you. Through the dark hours of the night, when you wake in the stillness the holy Name will surround you, and as you commend yourself again to sleep the Name of Jesus will refresh you. This is why one Orthodox monk said that when he discovered the Jesus Prayer he felt like the man in the Gospel who had found the pearl of greatest price.

Some have testified to seeing a divine light as they have prayed the Prayer; others to feeling the surge of a new energy within them or the awareness of a warmth and radiating heat. These are but symptoms—the important thing is that the Name of Jesus is enthroned within the interior cave of the heart, for there is the centre of life, love, light and warmth. The second great commandment of Jesus is, 'You shall love your neighbour as yourself.' It is the one whose heart is aflame with the love of Jesus who can effectively radiate compassion and stretch out a hand in practical help to those in need.

These words make clear that what is commonly called the Hesychast Way is not only the Jesus Prayer of quiet tranquillity, but is the life of love and intercession that will flow naturally and simply by the power of the Holy Spirit when once the Jesus Prayer is established and rooted in the heart—making it truly a prayer of intercession.

CHAPTER 10

THE JESUS PRAYER AND THE CHURCH'S PRAYER

Bishop Simon writes:

Discoverers of the new love

Among those people with a 'family likeness' whom I mentioned earlier, some of the most striking were the pioneers and explorers on the edge of the world of faith in which they had grown up, a place to which perhaps many more of us are being called today. I met many such people through my work with the CMS.

These were people who grew up as eager disciples in their own faith but also as ready seekers after truth wherever it might be found. There was a Muslim garage mechanic (whom I shall call 'B') in an Asian city, who as a schoolboy had been a keen student of his faith. He went to argue with a Scottish missionary about discrepancies between the stories of Jesus in the Gospels and in the Qur'an, which he was studying in Arabic. The missionary was astute enough to tell him that he should read the Gospels in the original language, and offered to teach him New Testament Greek. By the time B had mastered it, the missionary had departed, but B was soon hooked on the Gospels and then the epistles. He was fascinated by the notion of *agape* love, and became particularly attracted to 1 Corinthians 13 and supremely to John's Gospel. He took up the theme of Jesus as the embodiment of the divine *agape*, which he called 'the new love'. Later he gathered Muslim friends around him and they prayed in their usual way, kneeling, touching their heads on the ground (in the way that, long ago, Eastern monks whom the prophet Mohammed met had done) and chanting prayers or verses from the Qu'ran. But B's followers chanted verses from the New Testament on which they had meditated together. B's expositions of the significance of Jesus's enactment and gift of *agape* through the Holy Spirit were quite rabbinic in style, with complex textual arguments drawing on the whole Bible. Some of these were broadcast on a Christian radio station and certainly fascinated many of his own people. I suggested that he might get some theological training, but he eschewed Western ways of thinking as too alien and 'analytical'. The nearest he could get was Dostoevsky, whom he loved reading and whom he found capable of penetrating deeply into our Western malaise, our 'disintegration', and yet of pointing to the possibility of a new integration in Christ's love.

A fascination with 'the new love' expressed and released in Jesus the Messiah characterized many others whom I came across in different parts of Asia—people like T, a student of Christ from the Indian part of Kashmir, whose first encounter with the theme came when he picked up a copy of, once again, John's Gospel on a visit to the Church of North India Cathedral in Delhi. He went on to have a dream in which Jesus called him to preside over a 'committee' that was to be the first indigenous Christian movement in Kashmir. In the dream, Jesus was in the chair to initiate the new church, but he wanted to hand over to T. T also developed a gift for preaching and giving readings in public places from the Sermon on the Mount, which again spoke very vividly and directly even to some of the most warrior-like people living in the area, for whom the ethical teaching of Jesus often seems to have a real fascination. The violent reaction that the teaching could also arouse afterwards led to the crushing of the movement for the time being, but the magnetic appeal of the message was still clearly there. T has continued to become a man deeply possessed by the love of Christ, seeking to live in his presence and drawing others to him.

Down in the foothills towards the Serai (the plains) in Nepal, Indrabahadur, a devout Hindu, was one of the most outstanding prophetic figures I have ever met. Someone had given him a Nepali New Testament, and *his* reading of the Sermon on the Mount led to his being drawn closer and closer to the person of Jesus. His dedication to the Kingdom and the Way of Jesus had a strong influence on his brother, the village headman, and some close friends, and so generated a whole movement for self-help in the village. He initiated the handing over by the richer villagers of pieces of land for the landless, and, helped by a visiting volunteer from a development agency, the draining of the infertile land in the flood valley below. Then he created a communal grain store and a tool bank and began a specific service of caring for the local widows. He founded a group called the 'Society with a Small Vision' to help direct this change in the village. He drew on the help and friendship of Andrew Bulmer, a CMS mission partner (now with TearFund) who became his close friend and ally, supplying him with pumps and technical help. The new movement flowered and began to bear remarkable fruit in a change in the whole quality of life and relationships in the village. But suddenly and tragically Indrabahadur was killed as he rode his bicycle on his way to pick up some machinery. He was knocked over by a juggernaut lorry, thus, as Andrew commented, symbolizing for ever the precarious courage and vulnerability of an inspired champion of the poor.

One of the people who caught my imagination, through some research that I did in Nigeria, was a prophetic woman leader, Ibribina—a trader who in 1910 emerged with a message of one 'Jesu Krisi', a spirit being who had possessed her in the back of a mission church far away up the Niger. She introduced new songs and dances. She waved a Bible over the people to cleanse them from evil powers. But—what was far more significant—she went back and took instruction from the local CMS missionary which gradually enabled her to read and translate and interpret the Gospels in the Isoko language.

She came to see in 'Jesu Krisi' a new love, a new all-pervasive Spirit power, the possibility of a new people, a fellowship of the unlike, bonding together all 'tribes', all ethnic groups, both black and white, into a new society. Here the rich would care for the poor and the strong for the weak, in what was to be a new heaven and a new earth. Other leaders joined her and eventually thousands of people flocked in. In Europe the First World War was raging. This meant that CMS had to retrench. Only one inspired young missionary could make occasional visits to Ibribina's area. The movement thus grew vastly, drawing in the young of all ethnic groups and provoking conflicts with the elders, to whom the young adherents of the new movement seemed to be rebels introducing dangerous ideas. From the old people whom I interviewed I still picked up echoes and rhythms from the songs and dances of that miraculous time of hope, when they were young and were suddenly joined in one with all their contemporaries of the different ethnic groups in the area in a rapidly growing, mutually supportive fellowship. Then, in 1919, missionaries came in to tidy it all up and regularize things. Ibribina was assigned a role as a matron in a teacher training college, a role change that she never seemed to resent. Many of the other inspired leaders were sacked, however, for having more than one wife, and others were sent away to be properly trained. The mission agencies, after all, were shaping and training the new church to fit in with the wider colonial world. A much more individualized, spiritualized faith seemed appropriate along with a largely utilitarian education. Ever since Ibribina's time, African prophets and new church movements in that area have been trying in various ways to recover her original version of Christ's model for humankind.

The quest for the divine love of all these pilgrims, and so many others whose stories I would love to tell, led them to an encounter with the One in whom that love, which had already touched them within their own worlds of faith, became fully embodied—the wounded Messiah. People of all faiths, and sometimes of no specific faith at all, have an awareness of that love which gleams through the myriad patterns of differing cultures. And it is the two aspects of their discovery that lie at the heart of true worship.

The first aspect is a vision of the goal of humanity—of the harmony and right ordering of life, the *shalom*, the all-enfolding peace and joy that Jesus called the Kingdom. Drawing on the whole tradition of Jewish prophecy, he depicted it as a great feast with God—the marriage of heaven and earth. For all the seekers I have described, this vision is personified in the presence of the risen Jesus, the Christ in the midst, with those who surround him having their part in him through his Spirit within them all. The living Christ unites them all to himself.

The second is that they are given strength for the journey, a journey with Christ that will follow in the way of his cross, the way of forgiveness and of forgiving, the way of constant repentance and turning, the way of prayer and yearning. Above all, it is the way of obedient service and self-giving, which witnesses to the reality of that ultimate Kingdom. Into this way the worship brings them as they reach out in prayer, and sends them out as they go into action.

The new love in worship

A friend of mine once described how, when he was staying in a large South American city for a conference, early one evening he decided to go for a walk from his hotel in the surrounding area. Somehow he lost his way and stumbled into a rather seedy collection of huts and shacks on the outskirts of the city. He was on the edge of a *favela* (the equivalent of all the shanty towns or other makeshift settlements that spring up on the edges of large towns in the Two-Thirds world). There was quite a stink from the open drains over which plank-bridges led to little huts. By the doors he saw women looking pre-maturely old and, playing around them, undernourished pot-bellied children with bright, eager eyes. Then he passed a slightly larger hut, nearer the road, outside which a lively group of men and youngsters seemed to be putting together a small car from a variety of old parts. He stopped to talk to them and soon they were plying him with questions. He told them that he was there for a Christian conference. They were quite excited. It turned out that they were all members of a house church that met just there, which was going to make use of this car they were making. One of the men was the pastor and he invited my friend in for their communion service.

He crossed the planks with them and they gathered in one half of the hut. Through the sacking curtain that hid the rest, little faces peeped at the stranger. The pastor put on a rough white cloth cut like a poncho and stood behind a table with the rest gathered round. Then he prayed wonderfully and the others joined in with petitions, praying for my friend's family at home as well, and they sang accompanied by two guitars and some pipes. They all embraced my friend as they shared the Peace. When it came to the great Thanksgiving prayer, all spoke responses and the pastor improvised a rejoicing prayer over the bread and wine. It seemed to my friend that the roof opened up and all heaven surrounded them. They glimpsed themselves as part of a society where one day all the peoples of the earth would care for each other, all the good things of the world would be shared—where everyone would have their part to play and their contribution to make and all would have enough to eat. In the Confession, all had spoken freely and some wept. Now forgiveness prevailed. All sang and shouted alleluias. The bread and the wine were shared and the blessing given. They then escorted my friend back to near his hotel.

He felt he had never understood the Eucharist (or Communion or Lord's Supper) so well. Now he saw that, once again, Christ was the bridge between heaven and now. He puts his arms around us to take us into the final banquet where all will have their honoured place. By his grace he heals and cleanses us to strengthen us with this food. And so we in turn can become the bridge for those around us to a more abundant life, going out to put relationships right, to love and to serve one another as we have done at the feast, full of happiness that we are on our way!

I have to say that Orthodox worship, far more than our own, conveys so powerfully this sense of already being part of the world to come, with the icons of those who have gone ahead of us around and our own worship mingling with the worship of heaven and the absolutions and blessings and great intercessions—in which, to my surprise and joy, I have suddenly heard the names of my own family included—and the whole borne along on a flood of glorious sound. Eternal life seems to be breaking in here and now. Christ is both the Way and the End, in endless alternation.

But perhaps supremely it is in the churches of the poor that we experience the reality of coming home to Jesus' presence and of his empowering for the journey of discipleship. I have certainly found this in the little congregations of often unsupported and vulnerable groups of people in our inner cities and council estates with their often-heroic faith! I remember a congregation in a rather isolated and deprived estate, dominated by gangs of aimless young people and by just one or two disturbed and disturbing families. In a small church, a group, mostly elderly or quite young, all unemployed, gathered for little Lent meetings with their parish priest and a gifted woman missioner. These two proposed to have a kind of 'audience with God' like an audience with the Pope—only for this they put a small child holding a candle to sit in the middle. Then they invited the people to say anything they wanted to God.

There was such an immense silence that you could have thought it wasn't going to work. One elderly man said he wasn't going to play games and sat outside the group pointedly. But gradually and tentatively the questions came. They started rather broadly and then closed bit by bit on the more intimate and personal. So someone began with asking when the flats at the top of the estate would stop being boarded up, and someone else asked about how the burglaries could be stopped. But then a woman muttered the question, 'Will Len [her ex-husband] ever come back to me?' Another asked how her children could be kept from 'going wrong'. And gradually and more confidently the lonely questions poured in. At the end a young girl asked suddenly, 'If I'm so awkward, why did you make me?' After a pause, even the old man's voice suddenly broke in earnestly, ''Oo *are* you?'

Of course, the questions were in a sense unanswered. But they went on being articulated in that strange stillness that seemed at first an absence but then was somehow filled with presence. And before each other in that presence, those in the circle had uttered things that none of them would ever have voiced even perhaps to themselves, let alone to each other. Their questions were suddenly transformed into some kind of broken offering, as if they were like the alabaster jar of ointment which, not long before Jesus' death, a woman broke open and poured over his feet (Mark 14:3–9). The old man expressed something of the answer that Jesus' resurrection was to bring as he looked round at them all and said at the end, 'The 'ope I see is you!' It would be true to say that that group, indeed that church, was never quite the same afterwards. It was the small but costly and precious beginning of a process that was to bear fruit there much later. The seeds had been sown of a precarious movement of hope that would flower in days to come as, more and more, those people began to sense that 'Christ is among us' and to move towards his fulfilment.

Holding two moments together: the Jesus Prayer and the Lord's Prayer

For Orthodox believers, the Jesus Prayer is the strongest means of growth towards union with God apart from the sacrament itself. The Jesus Prayer gives us a direct awareness of the presence of Christ and of the wholeness of life in communion with the Trinity, into which he will bring us all as soon as we invoke his name in the power of the Spirit. Then the petition to Christ to draw us through our brokenness into his wholeness encapsulates the whole meaning of the Eucharist and thus of all Christian worship—the entry into the 'new love' and our growth into that love. The monks and nuns let the recitation of it flow through their consciousness throughout their days and nights. Even through their times of formal worship, the Prayer runs on within them. It leads them into the depths of Communion itself. In this way it becomes a kind of instilling into us of the content of the Lord's Prayer.

The Lord's Prayer (Luke 1:1–4; Matthew 5:9–13), after all, is also a holding together of the two 'moments' of worship 'in Christ'— coming home through him and journeying with him (see page 58 above). First there is the opening cry of 'Father' or 'Our Father', surely an echo of Jesus' own 'Abba', the intimate relationship with our Father and Mother God. This is the relationship that he won for us in the place where he used this name, Gethsemane—and supremely at Golgotha. And at once follow the great petitions essentially fulfilled for us already in his death for us and in his risen presence: 'Made holy be your name!' (in all the earth, when every knee shall bow, Philippians 2:10); 'Let come your Kingdom!'; and, in the words in which Matthew's version fills this plea out (Matthew 5:10), 'Let your will come to pass as in heaven also on earth'. This is the first 'moment'.

Then comes the second 'moment', a yearning plea for the little flock still on its precarious journey: 'Give us this day…' (Matthew 5:11), or 'each day…' (Luke 11:3), 'our *epiousion* bread'—a mysterious Greek word that could be used to mean 'tomorrow's' bread but is more likely to mean (according to early commentators) 'bread of the future or the last day'. 'Forgive us our debts…' (Matthew 5:12), or 'sins…' (Luke 11:4), 'as we forgive our debtors; do not bring us into (too great) a testing, but deliver us from (the) evil (one).' The essential way forward on our journey to the Kingdom consists in continuous giving and receiving of forgiveness. Nourish us (on the journey) and hold us through the terrible darkness!

In some early texts of Matthew's Gospel and in an early Christian (second-century) manual of instruction called *The Teaching of the Twelve Apostles*, there is added to the Lord's Prayer a characteristically Jewish ending called a doxology, that is, a 'giving of glory' of the kind Jesus is very likely to have used. It would have been strange for him to end the Prayer quite as abruptly as Luke or some Matthew texts do. The ending which in Christian tradition has been widely adopted, therefore, is, 'For the kingdom and the power and the glory are yours for ever.' This fuller version may well be nearer the original form of the Prayer, with Luke's and other shorter versions being adapted more for Gentile readers. This fuller ending returns to the homecoming to God, the arrival in his presence and entry into his Kingdom from which the prayer begins. The journey is then contained within the homecoming, repentance and longing within thanksgiving, the Kingdom 'not yet' within the Kingdom 'now' and the 'no' within the 'yes'! As Jesus often says in John's Gospel, 'The hour is coming and is now here…' (for example, John 5:25). Jewish prayer so often began and ended in thanksgiving and adoration, and the Lord's Prayer in this form does the same. For this reason, I always end the Jesus Prayer with the words, 'Lord Jesus Christ, Son of God', returning to where I began, that is, to 'standing in the presence of his glory with rejoicing!' (Jude 1:25).

Holding together these two moments of what I have called 'homecoming' and 'journeying' may have been more important than precise wording. So perhaps it is good that we have these two versions of the Lord's Prayer because they help us to do just that. There is, of course, no version of the prayer in Mark or in John.

Matthew 5:9–13 seems (like its setting, the Sermon on the Mount) almost to be an arriving home already in the final incoming of the Kingdom. Jesus is asking God to reveal his glory and usher in his reign as if they were round the corner. 'The bread of the world to come' (Athanasius' translation of *epiousion*—the word for 'daily' in 'daily bread') is apt. It could mean essentially the bread we *share*, the shared bread of the final feast in heaven. And Matthew says, 'Give us this bread of the last day, this bread of heaven, *now*': 'Give us *today* our *epiousion* bread!'

Luke's shortened version, like his setting for the giving of the prayer (Luke 11:1–4) is more of a prayer on the journey, for the 'iron ration' of grace each day on the way: 'Give us *each* day our *epiousion* bread.' The whole Luke/Acts narrative is a journey—a journey on the way from Bethlehem to Jerusalem and on to the ends of the earth. So perhaps the two versions emphasize the two poles of prayer and worship, joyful arrival in the presence of God, and longing and yearning in repentance and intercession for his fulfilment. And perhaps we particularly need to recover the rich corporateness of both versions of the Prayer (for example, in Matthew's version the use of 'Our Father') and the expectation of both, but especially Matthew's sense of homecoming already.

Above all, we need the fusion of homecoming and journey that is there in the Prayer and in the Jesus Prayer and in Jesus himself—'the Kingdom in himself'. Whenever that happens in worship and prayer, people are at once attracted to the universal Love. I remember an act of worship organized by a young woman I know in a large, dark, Victorian Gothic church. Many candles were lit. There were readings from the Bible and some from poetry and writings of saints, all interspersed with long silences and Taizé and Iona songs (the two great centres of good worship that attract seekers in plenty). In the heart of the service were sustained periods of recitation of the Jesus Prayer by one voice, first a woman's, then later a man's, as at the monastery. There was an introductory meditation but no sermon as such. Many of those who came, and sat on chairs or knelt on prayer stools, were people (as many men as women, and even more young than old) from the fringes of the Church or right outside it altogether. They were happy and wanting more of this transcendent love, which touched them at a deep level.

And I remember a great service in Guildford Cathedral with the theme 'The Prayer and the Passion' where we meditated on the Lord's Prayer being enacted in the Passion, the events of Christ's suffering and death. The striking paintings of Kathy Priddis, wife of the Bishop of Warwick and gifted artist, comprising her own 'Stations of the Cross', surrounded us. At the end the whole congregation sang Cliff Richard's inspired setting of the Lord's Prayer to the tune of 'Auld Lang Syne'. Its tune, with that strange aura of a secular ritual, evokes time past and time present being gathered up into one meeting-point, in a way that is both nostalgic and curiously anticipatory. Arms are crossed and hands linked and people sway to the rhythm in a circle as though they were reaching out towards some kind of wholeness. I was startled at the choice and then, as the many voices took it up, I was moved by what Cliff Richard had called 'The Millennium Prayer'. I was moved not least by the elusive but none the less universal and instinctive upsurge of the heart that the Lord's Prayer ought always to inspire, and which somehow the writers had caught perfectly in setting it to this tune. They had even had the nerve to add to the doxology at the end this bold yet utterly fitting verse, finishing with a repeated 'Amen'.

Let all the people say 'Amen' in ev'ry tribe and tongue.
Let ev'ry heart's desire be joined to see the kingdom come.
Let ev'ry hope and ev'ry dream be born in love again.
Let all the world sing with one voice, let the people say 'Amen'.

Paul Field and Stephen Deal © 1998 Meadowgreen Music/
EMI Christian Music Publishing/Stephen Deal Music/CopyCare

Every word of it rang true on that occasion in Guildford and filled out the 'Amen' with an amazing blend of joy and longing.

CHAPTER 11

THE JESUS PRAYER IN SICKNESS AND HEALING

Brother Ramon writes:

A few years ago I wrote an article for BRF on the use of the Jesus Prayer for healing. The reason for writing it was that I had found not only that its use had brought me into a deeper awareness of God's activity in my spiritual and mental life, but that it had physical repercussions which enhanced a certain relaxation and tranquillity of body. After all, we are a psychosomatic whole, and holistic medicine and practice is now a growing orthodoxy within the medical profession.

As a result of the article, I heard from people who were themselves experiencing a similar pattern, and one letter gave me particular joy because of the evident relief that the writer had experienced almost immediately. He had read the article just before entering hospital for eye surgery. Following the actual operation he had to lie on his front for some hours each day, keeping his head quite still.

He feared that he would find this very hard, but in the event he found that by remembering and practising the Jesus Prayer, not only did the time pass positively (and quickly!) but it indicated God's loving concern for him in his particular need. He saw this as a providential grace, and so he continues the practice.

Then something more radical happened to me in a serious diagnosis in my own life, calling for radiotherapy and manipulative hormonal treatment. I have known dark periods of pain and difficulty, yet never without the constant and deeper help of God, and constant practice of the Jesus Prayer. Indeed, in writing such words about the diagnosis, it is only honest to say that the depths of mystical awareness and love of God have been increasingly profound. I am also writing like this not to say that the use of the Jesus Prayer in sickness is less effective than I had thought but to affirm that I now find that its direction need not be towards physical healing (though that may well be included), but in a more spiritual dimension in our own and others' lives.

I would also add a qualification, and say that during times of radical, distracting pain or physical exhaustion and loss of concentration, it is best to return to the simple and basic Prayer, which does not demand the employment of thought processes. When Peter was sinking beneath wind and waves after his courageous step of faith on the waters of the lake of Galilee, he could only cry out in simple and utter desperation, 'Lord, save me!' (Matthew 14:30).

The healing variation of the Jesus Prayer

But supposing we are dealing with the ordinary pains and sicknesses of our everyday, sometimes robust and sometimes frail, existence. Let me commend the healing variation, as it may be of some help to you as it has been to me and others. I shall describe the variation first, and then to go on expound its meaning. The variation is an extension of the simple, basic Prayer and is fourfold:

Lord Jesus Christ
Son of God
Let your healing flow down
upon me;

Lord Jesus Christ
Son of God

Let your healing spring up
within me;

Lord Jesus Christ
Son of God
Let your healing love
enfold me;

Lord Jesus Christ
Son of God
Let your healing power
flow through me.

It may be worth printing the words on a card to place before you during a prayer session until you know them thoroughly, for in this context practice does make perfect, since it is a matter primarily of the heart.

Relevance and meaning for healing

As we have seen, the Jesus Prayer is an ancient and holy form of words, but the above variation is specifically pointed towards spiritual or physical healing. It is not a cajoling or begging prayer, trying to persuade a reluctant God to grant a desperate petition. Indeed, it asks rather that God's loving will may be embraced so that his saving and healing power is manifested—whatever that may mean in any particular situation. And it may not mean healing of a physical kind.

If sin is forgiven, the heart set upon God and the whole being waiting and open, then those barriers that keep God's grace at bay will be breached, and floodgates will open, admitting the healing river of love into the dry places of the soul.

We may begin with a session of the Jesus Prayer in its basic form until you feel ready to move into using the healing variation. Let me explain its various aspects:

'**Let your healing flow down upon me**': This is directed to Christ as *Pantocrator*—the Mighty One, the transcendent Christ who gazes into the believer's heart, as depicted in paintings on the dome of an Orthodox church or an icon. We may also contemplate the ever-deepening love flowing from the Father's heart, carrying life and fertility wherever it flows. We ask that this transcendent blessing, this cleansing river, may flow over and into us, bringing healing, life and peace.

'**Let your healing spring up within me**': God's Holy Spirit dwells within us, and our bodies are the temples of the Spirit, awaiting the rising springs of restorative powers that already reside within. This plea is directed towards the immanent Christ—the interior, indwelling mystery of Christ within, the 'hope of glory' (Colossians 1:27). The image is of a bubbling spring of healing water, a gentle, murmuring stream which, when the rubble is cleared, will spring up into every crevice of our being: 'Out of the believer's heart shall flow rivers of living water' (John 7:38).

'**Let your healing love enfold me**': If Christ is transcendent *above* us and immanent *within* us, he also completely surrounds us, caressing and holding us within himself, like protected children within the embrace of their mother. This is not a regress to the protecting womb for fear of the wicked world, but a retreat into the divine love so that, sustained and restored, we may return to the world as witnesses to God's embrace.

'**Let your healing power flow through me**': God's healing power does not stagnate in an interior lake with no outlet. Love always flows, and we are channels of its communication. If we experience the forgiving, healing and peace of God, then we shall become channels of blessing to others. The indwelling Spirit will flow through us and affect those around us, either physically or through prayers, joy and compassion.

Return to the basic Jesus Prayer

The use of this fourfold variation presumes that you will return to the basic Prayer. In any case, as I mentioned above, if you are seriously ill and cannot cope with the varied form, it would be best to stay with the familiar, simple form, casting yourself unreservedly upon God's mercy as I had to do, crying out, 'Lord Jesus Christ, Son of God, have mercy on me, a sinner.'

God knows our need, and he looks for a penitent spirit rather than liturgical excellence. In any case, the Jesus Prayer is simply part of the Church's rich life of prayer and adoration. It expresses humankind's yearning and response to the Spirit of God. It is part of the deep river of prayer that flows from the fecundity of grace through the cosmic order, and returns to the heart of God, our ultimate home and rest.

CHAPTER 12

HERMIT AND BISHOP PRAYING TOGETHER: A UNIFYING FELLOWSHIP AND JOY

Bishop Simon writes:

I was on a visit from Coventry to Volgograd (previously Stalingrad), with John Petty, then Provost of our Cathedral, exploring a link that had been established during the Second World War. On our arrival we were greeted by their Dean and by Archbishop German ('Herman'), who was a man of exceptional vision derived partly from the experience of having been bishop for the Orthodox in Berlin, and thus encompassing a wider view of things than many in the hierarchy at that time. At dinner he spoke of his longing to develop a Christian hospital and a Christian university. But one even greater priority loomed larger and seemed even more elusive: 'We really need most of all,' he said to me, 'a new Optino.'

He was speaking of a famous Russian monastery that became a place of pilgrimage for a number of intellectuals and writers and for a large number of people of all backgrounds towards the end of the 19th century, and for that last period of intellectual and spiritual flowering in Russia before 1914. The real source of Optino's attraction were three successive *staretsi* or elders (a title going back to the *Abba* or *Amma*—'Father' or 'Mother', sometimes misleadingly translated Abbot or Abbess—of the fourth- and fifth-century Desert hermits). The most famous of these three holy men was

Amvrosy. Dostoevsky made him the model for Father Zosima in the *The Brothers Karamazov*, and Tolstoy (whom he found rather more wearing) also visited him.

I was struck by the fact that a whole church, or indeed a whole society, could look for its inspiration to people of prayer in a great desert (or forest, in Russia) tradition going back centuries. Such people could be attached to monasteries—rather as Brother Ramon was at Glasshampton, while living a largely solitary life—and could then at some stage make themselves accessible to visitors seeking counsel. This pointed to a fundamental need of the whole Church since the very first days when people fled to the desert. The monastic movement first emerged as a critique, an alternative model of society. Apart from the emphasis on celibacy and the absence of families, there was a living out of the ideal of the New Testament Church—the sharing of food, wealth and property, each working for the good and caring for the needs of the others—and a fellowship of the unlike in which there were no barriers of race, class or nationality, where forgiveness prevailed, and where the least was the greatest and the leaders genuinely the humble servants of all. It could also suggest, as in the radical wing of the Reformation, the future goal of the Church and indeed of humanity itself, a community in which all gifts and needs are shared in peace and justice and in harmony with creation, and all life and creativity flows into mutual love and the worship of God.

I am sure that Brother Ramon was right to be fascinated by the idea of the hermit (*eremos* in Greek—linked to *eremia*, desert) and the bishop (*episcopos*, 'overseer'). The two forms of Church they represent surely need each other if they are to be true to the ideal of the Kingdom community and to the shared risen life that the Holy Spirit keeps struggling to recreate and renew. The divide between two forms of the Church, institutional and communal, that emerged towards the end of the third century was critical, and has arguably proved so for the Church in the East, in Russia and in the West ever since. In the Orthodox Church, as in Byzantium and then in Russia, there was some recognition of the need for a reintegration of the spiritual and the more secular dimensions of the Church in the development of the practice of appointing bishops drawn from the ranks of the monks—and that there could be, if rarely, joint monastic communities made up of men and women living side by side. But a marked gulf so often arose between a hierarchical church bound up very closely with the State and the prophetic and spiritual monastic communities and solitaries living in the desert or in the forest. In the West, the Eastern-inspired Celtic church drew its vitality and the inspiration for its mission from monastic communities and solitaries, with bishops far less significant in many ways, and was arguably the last expression of a fusion of the spiritual and the more loosely institutional.

In our own churches today, we are desperately in need of a far greater integration of the spiritual and contemplative with the organization and its structures. We are far from attaining to that sense of 'the Spirit in the wheels' of Ezekiel's vision (Ezekiel 1:15–21) in which the whole organization and administration of the Church is rooted in a culture of forgiveness, of the release and use of each member's gift in shared life and in true worship. This could only arise if the whole Church experienced an overwhelming movement of deep, strong prayer through which the divine love in Christ through the Spirit could make itself felt, reshaping our life and sending us out into radical action. Then we would see the full meaning of Dietrich Bonhoeffer's two requirements for a reconstituted Church—prayer and action!

An added obstacle in the whole of Western culture is undoubtedly what T.S. Eliot called, in a famous essay ('The Metaphysical Poets'), the 'dissociation of sensibility', which he suggested had emerged during the period of the Enlightenment, the Industrial Revolution and the Romantic movement. This was a separation of reason from emotion, through which we have lost so much of our capacity to feel our thoughts or to think our feelings. Our very critique of our present social order and our search for an economic pattern that can transcend capitalism and make any real sense of the seemingly self-contradictory notion of a so-called 'social market' are greatly hindered by this disability.

The simplest and most evident symptom of our condition is the conduct of church 'business' at any level from synod or assembly to local church council or its equivalents. A transient prayer or Bible study at best, or even an occasional quiet day, is followed by discussions and debates from which the stream of the Spirit could often appear to be totally excluded. The greatest difficulties are found in our attempts (and I speak very much from my own experience of failure) to bring together the handling of conflict and the struggle for the control of power with a strong relationship with Christ crucified and risen and a submission to the leading of the Spirit in all our affairs. In this critical situation, the 'spirituality' advisers' within Anglican dioceses, as well as the religious communities and (perhaps most significant of all) the hermits and solitaries, who could be the very sources of our recovery, are in danger of being relegated to the margins of our organizations, to provide us with an optional extra for those whose 'hobby' is prayer. Perhaps the predominant use of the difficult term 'spirituality' is itself a giveaway. It suggests buried springs or perhaps ornamental fountains, rather than the central stream of our life.

We are in our whole consciousness deeply divided. Of course, this has always been part of the human condition, but our own contemporary culture deepens our inability to achieve spiritual integrity. In the times in which I have been so privileged to share with my beloved Brother Ramon and the community at Glasshampton as a whole, as well as on the visits that Ramon and I paid at different times to the Orthodox Monastery of St John the Baptist, we both caught a glimpse of that reintegration of heart and mind, body, soul and spirit of which surely we shall discover the full meaning only in the world to come. And we saw then the possibility, which we hoped that this book may bring a little nearer to realization, that the Jesus Prayer itself might be one key provided for us by a long and rich tradition, a key drawn from the very beginnings of Christian life. We may start to learn to pray constantly, even without ceasing, 'with the mind in the heart'. The phrase itself implies a reintegration. We may be brought a little nearer to that integrity which God incarnate in Christ crucified continually re-presents to those who keep turning again and again to him in the power of the Spirit. And as we come to abide in the one true vine, our Churches themselves—Orthodox, Catholic, Protestant and Pentecostal—may come nearer to being unified inwardly, and then outwardly. They may show then that they have something infinitely precious to bring to the dialogue of all faiths and to the reintegration of humanity and indeed of the whole of creation.

Brother Ramon writes:

As I write, during the last month I have met with our five new novices, introducing them to the personal and corporate use of the Jesus Prayer. It was a joy to do this, and all the usual and necessary areas of group work, including the discipline and ease of posture, relaxation, breathing and mutual trust, have been involved. The group is moving into greater ease with its constituent parts, and one of the brothers has led the group in the initial repetition of the Prayer.

Grace building on nature

The development of this way of prayer depends on the way in which the group allows the Holy Spirit to work, and there are times when we set up barriers to such a spiritual flow. At best it is a matter of allowing grace to redeem and build on nature until one runs into the other in transcendent delight of fellowship. This is the found-ation upon which Jesus can make the following kinds of promises: 'If two of you agree on earth about anything you ask, it will be done for you by my Father in heaven. For where two or three are gathered in my name, I am there among them' (Matthew 18:19–20).

But in my praying with Bishop Simon, there was a minimum of preparation. The sense of being made ready and mutual communication in the Spirit was there from the beginning, and enabled us to focus down into the basic, necessary yielding of our ourselves to one another, so that the 'together' aspect led us into the deeper reaches of spiritual discernment. This meant that the praying of the Jesus Prayer every day, together and apart during our Glasshampton sharing and now in the actual putting together of this book, manifests the Spirit at work.

It was not just a matter of compatibility of natural temperament and the joy of simple, wholesome friendship, but an awareness of the Other the divine, indwelling Christ. It was rooted in evangel ical and catholic joy overflowing in human love, and included a call, a commission and a task to lead others into sharing in these chapters.

We ourselves do not know what the outcome will be, for we remain quite different personalities, and doubtless there will be quite different ways of understanding the same experience of grace that came to us both simultaneously. One of the factors during the Glasshampton week together was my experience of some physical pain, especially during the afternoons when Bishop Simon was able to go walking around the monastery. I say this because during both the morning sessions of prayer together and the afternoon sessions apart, I was aware of his loving concern for me. At this physical level it enhanced our common experience rather than detracting from its significance. He was given discerning grace to help me, and I was given sufficient grace to continue to receive what God had prepared for us.

I have been given a respite of God's healing power since that time, and we can both rejoice at this stage in our work together. It would be somewhat too personal and subjective to write like this if it were not for the fact that its consequence has been the impetus and stimulus to share with you, our reader, what God is sharing with us.

As God has led us through the years of evolving life and ministry within the fellowship of the Church, it has meant growing ecumenical contacts with our Roman and Reformed fellow Christians. This has reflected the pain of separation as well as the joy of a greater fullness within the whole. The continuing and growing relationship with Eastern Orthodoxy is part of the ecumenical scene, and all the churches are more socially aware, more compassionately involved, and more united in how witness is made in areas of peace and justice.

As two brother Anglicans, Bishop Simon and I are sadly aware of the Great Schism that separated the Eastern from the Latin Church of the West in 1054, and the further fragmentation of the Reformation during the 16th century. But we are also aware of a deeper unity, a more powerful dynamic, a revitalizing gospel life that the Holy Spirit is pouring into East and West, into Catholic, Reformed and Anglican churches today. It fills us with great hope as we see the light in each other's eyes, and share the joy in each other's hearts.

So when we have participated in a way of praying such as the practice of the Jesus Prayer over 25 years, and feel again that warm joy, that interior unity, that inward affirmation that comes from taking the prayer rope in our hands alone or with others, then there is need to offer thanks and praise for the ecumenical sharing that is involved.

The saving, forgiving, reconciling and healing power of the name of Jesus is the gospel foundation upon which the Church was born in Acts 2. It blazes the trail through the Gospel writings and epistles of the New Testament, into the world of the early, persecuted Church, into the deserts of Palestine, Syria and Egypt. There are times when sight is lost of its glory and it runs underground due to corruption of doctrine and practice. But always the Spirit of God stirs up his people, and revival and restoration lifts up the powerful name of Jesus again.

Can you imagine the joy with which John Cassian and his monk colleague moved among the Desert Fathers of the fourth century, observing and sharing their lives of gospel simplicity and prayer? Bishop Simon and I would like to see ourselves as similar observers.

John Cassian himself (c.350–c.435) was equally conversant with Latin and Greek, linking the Eastern and Western Christian worlds. John Chrysostom ordained him deacon around 400 in Constantinople, and he was sent to Rome, where he came to know Leo the Great and was ordained priest. He wrote his famous *Conferences* about his experiences and conversations with those who had gone to live in the deserts of Egypt and Palestine. The Rule of St Benedict quotes Cassian at length, and the *Conferences* have been read every evening in Western monasteries for generations. They contain the best of the spirituality of Origen and Evagrius, a mysticism of light and love, and the meditative prayer of the psalms with repetition of a short formula of prayer to still the mind.

Let us hope it is not too bold a claim to make that Bishop Simon and I are sharing and teaching the Jesus Prayer in our small corner of the Church, and that this leads the participants ultimately to the biblical hope and promise of union with God.

CHAPTER 13

THE 'BIG HULLO': THE JESUS PRAYER AND OUR FINAL UNION WITH GOD

Bishop Simon writes:

Brother Ramon and Archimandrite Sophrony

One of my favourite moments in that delightful piece of ascetic writing, *The Way of a Pilgrim* (the story of a Russian seeker who wandered through his country in the 1850s, discovering and then practising the Jesus Prayer), occurs not long after the death of the author's revered *staretz*, his 'elder' or spiritual guide. The poor pilgrim was trying, on his own, to read through an anthology of extracts from the Eastern Fathers on this way of praying. His elder had recommended it to him, and he had secured a battered copy. The *Dobrotolyubie* (or 'Lover of Beauty') was a Russian anthology of Orthodox writings on prayer through the centuries, translated from Greek. But alas, the pilgrim found, as others have found, that even trying to read it straight through was a bit too much. He simply couldn't find his way to the passages he needed most. He prayed and struggled desperately for a day and a night and then fell asleep. At once he dreamt that he was back with his dear old *staretz*, who began to explain the book to him and tell him which bits to read. When he failed to find one particular passage, the *staretz* turned to it for him and marked it in the margin with a piece of charcoal picked off the floor. When the pilgrim woke up, wondering if it really had been the old man, he found the book, which the night before he had tucked firmly under his pillow, lying open on the table at the place that was marked. The charcoal stick was lying beside it!

This story, like others describing how students of prayer are helped from beyond death by their former *staretz*, and how that *staretz* in turn would have been helped by his predecessor and so on, going right back to the Desert Fathers and Mothers, seems typical of Orthodox tradition. As I sit here in my attic study, I can look across to a photograph of my own revered 'Desert Father', Archimandrite Sophrony. 'He being dead yet speaketh' (Hebrews 11:4, AV), not least through his dear brothers and sisters in the monastery that he founded in this country. It is a place that both Ramon and I had visited on different occasions. It was there that I first really learnt to pray the Jesus Prayer. And beside me I can also see a shelf full of Ramon's books, one of which he gave me each time I saw him. On the chest that I use as an altar stands a card on which he wrote out the Jesus Prayer in Greek for me. As I pray it aloud, I can almost hear his voice chiming in. As the poet Henry Vaughan would say, 'I see them walking in an air of glory, Whose light doth trample on my nights and days...'.

Those who have inspired us, even if only through their books, surround us and urge us on. Already we catch glimpses of that 'Big Hullo' that Ramon spoke of to me just before he left us. He was so full of the sense that 'the best is yet to be'! Together he and Archimandrite Sophrony remind us that our little struggles in prayer and action, our daily journey to God, are a part of a movement towards the final homecoming of all creation. They beckon us on. At the end of Ramon's list of contents for this book, I found that he had suggested that there should be a last chapter written by both of us on *theosis*, or becoming one with God, a theme with which the Jesus Prayer has always been specially associated. He hadn't mentioned this but there it was written down. For Father Sophrony, this was undoubtedly central to his and to the entire Orthodox vision. I decided then that the best way to tackle it would be to show how it had emerged in his experience and his vision.

Father Sophrony's discovery

In Moscow and Paris

Archimandrite Sophrony (1893–1993), originally Sergei Sakharov, was certainly someone with an instinct for the transcendent, right from childhood days. As a young boy, brought up in a Russian Orthodox household, he learnt to pray for three quarters of an hour at a time without tiring. Indeed, it was then that he first became aware of the divine 'uncreated' light within and around him as he prayed, a phenomenon that had always been associated in Orthodox tradition with the active presence of the Holy Spirit. As an art student in war time, and then in the Russian Revolution, he came to reject the Christian view of God, as he understood it then as too particular and individualistic, too restricting. He remembered how, as he walked in a street in Moscow, he renounced the Christian framework. He subsequently struggled, through his painting and through a kind of yogic meditation in his studio, to discover the purely abstract Absolute, the divine ground and source of all life, of Asian religions.

Having emigrated to Paris in 1921, he seemed eventually to reach a kind of spiritual dead end and to feel himself lost in a void. It was then, this time in the streets of Paris, that he arrived at a startlingly new discovery. Quite suddenly and unexpectedly there dawned upon him an intensely vivid disclosure of the living God, blazing over him and through him, a revelation of the eternal and infinite 'I AM THAT I AM' (Exodus 3:22) incarnate in Christ, crucified and risen, and thus essentially personal in a way beyond all that Moses had known. He realized that God cannot be found by the questing intellect or by the imagination, but only by love deep within us, which responds to the divine Love. As he was enveloped in the cleansing and healing light of the triune God, revealed through the Spirit, he recognized the vast profundity and scope of this personal and relational God. He saw that within ourselves there is an immediate response, an answering capacity for relationship and personal communion, heart speaking to heart. In the person of Christ we have been shown what it really means to be human. Through his incarnation, his cross and his resurrection, the human and the divine have been brought together and made one. The human person becomes most true to itself when it is opened up to the divine and the infinite. The human person originally made in the image and likeness of God is forgiven, and, being restored to that image and likeness through Christ, is beginning to be raised up in him into the life of the Trinity.

As Sophrony studied in the newly formed Orthodox Theological Institute in Paris, the central insight of Orthodox theology became clear to him. As Irenaeus had put it in the second century, 'God became man that man might become divine'. From Athanasius onwards the Eastern Fathers had taken up this theme. Human nature could no longer be seen as closed and finished and static, but dynamic, shaped by its affinity and its relationship to God. Human beings were destined to grow and to ascend into communion with God, being joined by the Holy Spirit through Jesus Christ to the Father. The whole creation was being drawn onwards and upwards into God through the transformed minds and hearts of human beings brought 'into Christ'. Of course they would never cease to be creatures, but they would be creatures transfigured through sharing in Christ's own deified humanity through the Spirit.

It was all entirely biblical. The whole New Testament tells a story that centres on the assurance that the resurrection of Jesus makes him 'the firstborn of a large family' (Romans 8:29). It is all there in Romans 8, where the Spirit is drawing those who believe in Christ, and who live 'in the Spirit that raised Jesus from the dead'

(Romans 8:11), to be 'children of God and joint heirs with Christ' (Romans 8:17). Indeed, in 1 Corinthians 15, their final goal beyond death is to be united with him and to 'bear the image of the man of heaven' (1 Corinthians 15:49). In 2 Corinthians 3:18, 'all of us, with unveiled faces, seeing the glory of the Lord as though reflected in a mirror' (NRSV) are being changed 'into the same image from glory to glory... by the Spirit of the Lord' (NKJV). Again in John's Gospel, our whole destiny, since we have been given power to become the children of God (John 1:12–13), is that we should be with Jesus in his glory (John 17:20–24). John's first letter declares that 'we are God's children now, and it does not yet appear what we shall be, but we know that when he appears, we shall be like him' (1 John 3:2, RSV). This surely is the very heart of *theosis*.

On Mount Athos, in Paris and at the Monastery of St John the Baptist

Sophrony was still filled with a deep desire to learn *how* we can enter this growth into union with God. He felt he had not yet learned 'how to pray, how to have a right attitude towards God, how to overcome one's passions, and attain eternity'.[1] So, like many a Russian pilgrim before him, he resolved to travel to Mount Athos, to the Russian monastery of St Panteleimon, and to seek instruction from the prayer guides he would surely find there.

In the end, after some searching, he was not disappointed. In 1930, he found the person who could really help him. Saint Silouan (a Russian version of the New Testament name Silvanus), as he is now known, was then a relatively obscure member of the community when Sophrony stumbled across him, although some who knew him well had quite a respect for him. He had come himself to the monastery, as an almost illiterate peasant from Russia, on the same errand as Sophrony and so many others. His parents had been deeply godly people in their quiet, steadfast way, and he had been shaped by the kind of strong, simple peasant faith that Dostoevsky evokes so strongly (for example, in *The House of the Dead*). In Silouan, this faith developed strikingly into a passionate repentance of youthful follies and an intense and infinite longing for God. By the time Sophrony came to know him, he was astonished by the profound experience of God in Christ that had been given to this apparently simple, untutored man, which seemed by then, to Sophrony's amazement, identical with that of so many of the early ascetic Fathers.

Sophrony had the wisdom to perceive that he had found truths embodied in the prayer life of this humble monk that academic theologians and philosophers alone could not have shown him. He became Silouan's disciple, companion and scribe until his *staretz*'s death in 1938. In the years that followed, Sophrony stayed in the monastery. Through reflection and study and prayer, he continued to seek to explore the significance of his teacher. Eventually, after the war, Sophrony returned to Paris to write his findings into a biography of Silouan and an anthology of his meditations. He entitled it *The Undistorted Image*, the portrait of someone who had faithfully embodied 'the image and likeness' of God in a human being in such a way as to point us all towards our own eternal destiny.

Finally Sophrony crossed over to Britain, with some of the followers who had joined him in Paris, to start a new monastery in a former Anglican rectory in Essex. Here the truths he had received from Silouan could be embodied in the life of the community he formed.

The way down is the way up

The icon of St Silouan which was created in this monastery, where Father Sophrony had begun a new school of icon painting, tells the whole story in a another medium. I have one here among the icons in my little place of worship. The painter herself presented it to me on behalf of the community. In his book, Father Sophrony describes Silouan as tall, well built and proportioned, with bushy eyebrows and a full beard, and having a striking 'presence' in spite of his gentle self-effacingness. His face was less severe than photographs of him might suggest. 'His gaze was quiet and restful', although 'penetratingly intent', sometimes weary from wakefulness and weeping in prayer, sometimes lit by a radiance so striking that people could hardly look at him. There was a strange quality of both sadness and serene peacefulness about him. This is just how he appears in the icon.

The truth of the icon is the truth of his life and of his teaching as Father Sophrony gives this to us. The essential principle which in his whole being Silouan embodied and conveyed, the real secret of our journey towards union with God, was that 'the way down is truly the way up'. This is what comes through to us in all that Father Sophrony has so wonderfully described of him in his book, which since his canonization has been published in a new edition as, simply, *Saint Silouan, the Athonite* (St Vladimir's Seminary Press, 1999).

His exceptional powers of spiritual perception and his ardent longing for God, even before his arrival on Mount Athos, had shown him the depths of the reality of sin within himself, confronting him with a sensation of flames burning around him, demons that seemed to speak to him like people, and agonies of despair. Yet amazingly early in his time there, the Jesus Prayer, which every novice was instructed to say day and might, had already actually entered into his heart. The prayer had begun to flow through his inmost consciousness in a stream that never ceased. This often brought him temporary relief in his battle with 'the passions' of lust, fear and confusion or insidious pride that attacked him so strongly.

There was an amazing moment, as he stood by an icon of the Saviour at Vespers, when he was given an extraordinarily powerful and compelling vision of the living Christ, filling his whole being with 'the fire of the grace of the Holy Spirit'. A divine light shone about him and he was lifted out of this world and experienced some kind of 'new birth' as he felt 'the gaze of the joyous, all-forgiving, boundlessly-loving Christ' drawing this young novice to himself. Yet this was the prelude to months and years of nocturnal battles, of being assailed by wrong thoughts and imaginings, by crowds of demons, and by a stifling sense of abandonment by God. In all this time he was engaged in heavy, manual work, in corporate worship and in coping with community, with workers and with visitors. It was fifteen years before that strangest moment of all when, wearied and battered, he cried out to the Lord in the face of yet one more terrible attack, 'What must I do to stop the devils hindering me?' He received the somewhat discouraging answer, 'The proud always suffer from devils.' When he then asked how to be made humbler, he received in his heart the famous answer, 'Keep thy mind in hell and despair not.'

The paradox is that it was in that very moment that he actually received the key to the gate into the way onward and upward towards union with God. This amazing prescription was to transform him. The point is that he had been shown that the intense light of love and tender forgiveness given to him in the vision long before could only be received in humble surrender and acceptance of his incapacity for heaven. He had to let go any attempt of his own to save his life or any confidence that of himself he could save it. 'Those who try to make their life secure will lose it, but those who lose their life will keep it' (Luke 17:33). There was something here of the moment of truth experienced by Paul when God said to him, in answer to his plea to be rid of whatever was troubling him, 'My grace is sufficient for you, for my power is made perfect in weakness' (2 Corinthians 12:9).

Silouan had now been given a deep sense of self-despair and, simultaneously, an infinite trust and confidence in being constantly held in love and forgivenness. He knew then the secret that he could discern in the saints, the Desert Fathers and Mothers of old and in the long line of those who had prayed the Jesus Prayer since them through the centuries. It was the secret glimpsed by St Antony as he cried out, 'All shall be saved and only I shall perish', or St Seraphim of Sarov (1759–1832), who had lost the sense of grace he was once given and in apparent abandonment stood a thousand days on bare stone in the wilderness, invoking God to 'be merciful to him, a sinner', only for the light of the Spirit to shine in the end more powerfully than ever through his battered and frail form. And there were so many others. Their true confidence in grace was brought to birth not through ecstasies or dramatic visions but through a humility and self-loss that, none the less, were accompanied by a depth of faith in the hidden love that held them steadfast, though they were stripped of all else.

This is the humility of Christ in Gethsemane out of which he can cry 'Abba! Father!' (Mark 14:36). It is the thread of faith that holds him always on Golgotha in the face of apparent abandonment by God when he utters the words, 'My God! My God, why have you forsaken me?' (Mark 15:34). God is humility and he who would 'put on' God must be humble. Christ 'emptied himself', *wherefore* God has highly exalted him. Those who humble themselves will be exalted. The Greek word for Christ's 'emptying' or 'outpouring' of himself (Philippians 2:7) is *kenosis*. And God is this *kenotic* love into which we must all be drawn more and more. Even the persons of the Trinity are related to each other in this mutual *kenosis*. This was the way Silouan discovered into pure prayer and it is the essence of the Jesus Prayer itself and of the way of life into which it must lead us.

Further steps along this 'way down' towards *theosis* open out in Silouan and in Sophrony as his disciple from this point. Silouan was already known to be kind, hardworking and conscientious, someone to whom people could turn in need and who always seemed to respond in the same gracious manner. His prayer deepened, and he withdrew to Old Rossikon, a remoter, more desert place, for greater quiet. It was then that he began to realize that, as he often expressed it, 'our brother is our life'. In the depth of the heart he could discern how all humankind were bound up together with him in his own being. Just as Sophrony had perceived our affinity with the personal and relational nature of God, so he would learn from Silouan that this means that, like the Trinity, we are at the deepest level 'members one of another', not only within the Church but also within humanity as whole. In our prayer and in our shared life we must realize more and more fully this sense in which every person is our eternal brother or sister. Like the Desert Fathers, or like Isaac of Nineveh, hermit and bishop (d. 700), Silouan found that praying meant reaching out in spirit to touch with compassion animals, birds, insects, plants, creatures of sea and land, the whole torn fabric of God's creation.

After some time in Old Rossikon, Silouan was appointed steward in charge of the monastery's workshop at the mill. There, as he became responsible for a number of Russian peasant workers, he learnt increasingly what it meant to intercede for every person. 'To pray for people is to shed blood,' he often said. This powerful sense of praying for 'the whole Adam' (and Eve) and of our all being part of each other eternally, grew upon him. This brought him still closer to the mutual interdependence of the Trinity. Sophrony much later sought to give this reality fresh expression, first by forming a community in Paris, then by founding the monastery in England. He saw the monastic life as bringing us nearer to the realization of our kinship with the triune God, specifically through this mutual belonging. Even spiritual direction or counselling itself became an entering into another's life as they are drawn into yours.

As, in recent decades, we have come to see more clearly that masculinity and femininity are present in each person of the Trinity, it is surely significant that Father Sophrony later developed, in accordance with the intuitive wisdom of some ancient tradition in Eastern monasticism, a community for women alongside men. Indeed the *koinonia*, the communion, of the Trinity reaches out through the cross to generate a unity in difference, a fellowship of the unlike transcending all contrasts of temperament, class, culture and ethnicity. The possibility is created then of forming a community that can be the nucleus of a model of kenotic life in so many ways. But such a model can only be realized through constant acknowledgement of failure, constant repentance, confession and mutual forgiveness and thus an ever-deeper, trusting surrender through Christ to God. It is through self-despair and the receiving of grace *together* that we are drawn more and more into the life of the Trinity. As it has been said, the floor has to fall away rather than the roof being raised! As the community recites the Jesus Prayer together, this daily becomes more and more apparent.

In such a community (as in Father Sophrony's monastery), the Jesus Prayer could actually became the main liturgical 'office' said corporately. It flows on through every activity unceasingly. It is always an extraordinary fusion of praise and intercession. It touches all that the members of the community do. It is interwoven with every task they tackle and everyone they encounter and care for. For Silouan, it reached out beyond the community—beyond the wider circle of ordinary humanity, even—to all those alienated from themselves and from the rest of us and, even more, those who have deliberately alienated themselves from God. This reaching out in compassion became bound up with his root principle that we must above all 'love our enemies'. This became for him a cardinal theme in our growth into union with God in his limitless mercy.

After Silouan had received that summons to 'keep your mind in hell' he found himself not only praying for the living, especially for those inhabiting a living hell, but even crying out to God for the dead. He could not help himself. He could not bear to think of anyone languishing in outer darkness. 'Have mercy on me' or 'on us' becomes 'on all', on all suffering creatures, on all beings. To a brother who said with satisfaction, 'God will punish all atheists', Silouan answered, 'Would you be happy to see somebody burning in hellfire?'

'It can't be helped,' said the other. 'It would be their own fault.'

Silouan replied, 'Love could not bear that. We must pray for all.' From then on, to the end of his life, he became a great intercessor, characterized by his fervently compassionate prayer for all, accompanied at times by overwhelming tears at a time when the outer world was facing the onset of the Russian years of terror, the rise of fascism and the Holocaust. Here again in his prayer the love of God was poured out in the groaning of the Spirit within Silouan as he was caught up into the divine purpose. He experienced something of what it means to be united with the love of the Christ who has taken our wounds into the heart of heaven. In the midst of the Trinity he 'ever lives to make intercession for us' (Hebrews 7:25).

These were some of the ways in which Sophrony learnt from Silouan, and taught to us, how praying and living the Jesus Prayer together could enable us to come nearer to the reunion of all things in the world to come. Sophrony was to take all that he had been given through his beloved *staretz* and interpret it, setting it into the tradition of the Fathers and Mothers of old and giving it a modern philosophical framework. It led him into his own greatest insight as he yearned, through a deepening communion in the Spirit, to reach out to realize his mutual belonging with his fellow human beings, with his 'enemies' and with all created beings; and, within the inner stream of ceaseless prayer, out of self-despair and by grace alone, to be drawn into the life and action of the living God, as he prayed the Jesus Prayer together with his brothers and sisters in the community.

That same strong current was flowing though Ramon, especially in his last months and days. As we prayed the Prayer together, it took on more of the character of a stream flowing out into the ocean of love in which the whole creation will find its final homecoming.

In Father Sophrony's last year, he had appeared almost translucent as the veil separating him from the light of the coming day seemed to be growing thin. Ramon, so much younger when his final journey began, remained outwardly and strikingly his beloved, genial, earthly self, although in a hidden way he suffered mentally as well as physically as he had to face being snatched away from all the joy of his solitary life and the delight he took in the occasional visits of his friends in this world. Through all the ups and downs of those final months, as he sat up writing after all and then at length had to take to his bed, he increasingly recognized, reluctantly at first and not without fear or the grief of a kind of bereavement in reverse, that he had now to turn towards that eternal light which now and then kept shining out for him from beyond the dark. With tears, with laughter often, with pangs of anxiety and yet with his strongly recurring awareness of the presence of the risen Christ, he still held on to the Prayer he had enabled others to pray together with him. It was that very frail and lovable humanity, and yet the underlying impulse that kept resurging to look ahead to our ultimate goal and destiny, which made him such a special inspiration for me.

So, with Father Sophrony and with Brother Ramon in their differing approaches to the same essential Way, we are all moving towards that 'big hullo!' to which they pointed us, when the freedom and justice and wholeness for which all the earth cries out will finally enfold us, and we shall be gathered with unshadowed joy into the great feast of the life to come. Towards that day let us pray together *and live together* the prayer, 'Maranatha! Come, Lord Jesus!'

Lord Jesus Christ, Son of God, have mercy upon us! Amen.

Notes

1 It was Professor J.A.W. Bennett who first drew my attention to this early tradition of the 'young Prince of Glory,' the warrior, still echoed in Watts' first draft. Compare his further comment on this theme in 'Vision of a Rood' and other works in that fine book of his lectures, *Poetry of the Passion*, Oxford University Press, 1982.

2 A phrase used by Bruce Chilton, a New Testament scholar, as the title of his monograph of that name.

3 See extracts from his writings in *The Art of Prayer*, Igumen Chariton, Faber, 1966.

4 Father Sophrony quoted in a D.Phil. thesis on him written by Nicholas Sakharov for Oxford University to which I am indebted for some of the information given here.

BIBLIOGRAPHY

The most outstanding and easily accessible book is Kallistos Ware, *The Prayer of the Name: The Jesus Prayer in Orthodox Spirituality*, Marshall Pickering, 1989 and The Sisters of the Love of God, Convent of the Incarnation, Fairacres, Oxford, 1986.

A good practical book is Brother Raymond SFF, *Praying the Jesus Prayer: A contemporary introduction to an ancient method of contemplative prayer*, Marshall Pickering, 1988.

A rather more idiosyncratic, but attractive, book is Archimandrite Lev Gillet's book, *On the Invocation of The Name of Jesus by a Monk of the Eastern Church*, published by The Fellowship of St Alban and St Sergius.

Also by Archimandrite Lev Gillet is *The Jesus Prayer*, revised with a foreword by Kallistos Ware, St Vladimir's Seminary Press, 1987.

The famous little book *The Way of a Pilgrim* translated from the Latin by the Reverend R.M. French, first published in 1930 by Philip Allan, has been republished by SPCK, most recently in a paperback edition in 1973, and has since been reprinted a number of times.

The less valuable, but still interesting, sequel *The Pilgrim Continues His Way* was published by SPCK/Triangle in 1986.

A good little Protestant book on the Jesus Prayer is *The Jesus Prayer: learning to pray from the heart*, by a Lutheran author Per-Olof Sjögren, Triangle, 1986.

Archimandrite Sophrony has written on the Jesus Prayer in *His Life is Mine*, A.R. Mowbray, 1977. He has also written about St Silouan: *The Monk of Mount Athos*, St Vladimir's Seminary Press, 1973 and *Wisdom from Mount Athos*, St Vladimir's Seminary Press, 1975.

Another attractive book by a Russian Orthodox author of the nineteenth century is Bishop Ignatius Brianchaninov, *On the Prayer of Jesus*, translated by Father Lazarus, Element Books, 1987.

Another book written originally by an Orthodox nun for Anglican Benedictine nuns (with whom she stayed for fourteen years before moving to head her own small monastery) links up the insights of her own tradition with that of the West as expressed in St Therese of the Child Jesus and St Catherine of Genoa. This book is *The Jesus Prayer* by Mother Maria, published by Greek Orthodox Monastery of the Assumption, Whitby, North Yorkshire, YO22 4PS, 1972.

There is also a good little book by Irma Zaleski, a Polish Catholic who developed her praying of the Prayer in Canada: *Living the Jesus Prayer*, published by Gracewing.

Two attractive books which are now out of print, but obtainable from a library, are:

Tito Colliander, *The Way of the Ascetics*. The author was a Russian Orthodox layman who lived most of his life in Helsinki, Finland.

Alphonse and Rachel Goettman, *Prayer of Jesus—Prayer of the Heart*, translated by Theodore and Rebecca Nottingham, Paulist Press, 1991. This is a most attractive book of great power.

Finally, for delving more deeply into the history of the Jesus Prayer, there is Irenee Hausherr, *The Name of Jesus*, translated by Charles Cummings, Cistercian Publications, 1978.

Prayer ropes can be obtained from Orthodox Christian Books Ltd, Studio 7, Townhouse, Alsager Toad, Audley, ST7 8QJ.